HANDBOOK FOR
MENTAL HEALTH CARE
OF DISASTER VICTIMS

RAQUEL E. COHEN, M.D., M.P.H., is associate professor at the Harvard Medical School, superintendent of the Erich Lindemann Mental Health Center in Boston, and director for mental health and mental retardation in the Harbor Area, Boston, Massachusetts.

FREDERICK L. AHEARN, Jr., D.S.W., is chairman and associate professor of Community Organization and Social Planning at the Boston College Graduate School of Social Work.

HANDBOOK FOR MENTAL HEALTH CARE OF DISASTER VICTIMS

Raquel E. Cohen, M.D., M.P.H.
and Frederick L. Ahearn, Jr., D.S.W.

THE JOHNS HOPKINS UNIVERSITY PRESS
Baltimore and London

Copyright © 1980 by The Johns Hopkins University Press
All rights reserved
Printed in the United States of America

The Johns Hopkins University Press, Baltimore, Maryland 21218
The Johns Hopkins Press Ltd., London

Library of Congress Cataloging in Publication Data

Cohen, Raquel E
 Handbook for mental health care of disaster victims.

 Bibliography: pp. 115-21.
 Includes index.
 1. Disasters—Psychological aspects. 2. Crisis
intervention (Psychiatry) 3. Community mental
health services. I. Ahearn, Frederick L., joint
author. II. Title. [DNLM: 1. Disaster planning—
United States. 2. Community mental health services—
United States. WM30 C678h]
BF789.D5C63   362.2   80-81426
ISBN 0-8018-2427-3

When You Die, You Leave Your Things.
In This Case, Your Things Left You
and You Die a Little with Them.

Statement of tornado victim
Windsor Falls Locks, Connecticut
February 1980

CONTENTS

FOREWORD

The history of the mental health field in the twentieth century shows continual expansion of mental health knowledge and its application to diverse aspects of human problems. An important result of this expansion of knowledge has been greater understanding of the ways in which human beings—as individuals, as members of families, and as members of social communities—react to and cope with various types of stress.

Research on stress provides an important link between the scientific disciplines of anthropology, sociology, epidemiology, and biology. Scientists are interested in the physiologic mechanisms by which the organism adapts to the environment through mobilization of various adaptive systems, particularly the hypothalmic-pituitary-adrenal-cortical system, as discussed by Hans Selye, and the sympathetic nervous system, as outlined by Walter Cannon.

One important extension of this research has been the linkage of internal physiologic reactions to external stimuli, whether they come from the social environment or from the natural environment. Most of modern life has been concerned with changes in the immediate psychosocial environment due to changes in interpersonal relations, economic change, or loss and separation from loved ones. However, although modern man has increasingly freed himself by means of technology from the vicissitudes of natural disaster, this is not completely true. Famine, floods, plagues, and pestilence are far less common with us than they were with our ancestors, but we are not completely free of stresses coming from changes in our natural environment. Therefore, disasters due to natural conditions such as floods, earthquakes, and volcanoes still remain an important part of human experience and are logical events to study.

This study by Dr. Cohen and Dr. Ahearn therefore represents an important contribution to understanding human adaptation and stress. The natural disaster in Massachusetts provided a unique opportunity to study not only the impact this event had upon individuals and their families but also the ways in which mental health knowledge could contribute to a better mobilization of social and community resources, so as to minimize the adverse effects of this disaster upon mental health, social cohesion, and community resources.

The accumulation of knowledge in this area will have practical benefit both to other mental health workers and to the field of disaster research in general. It will also contribute to our knowledge of the ways in which the human organism interacts with its environment and the important interplay between biological and environmental factors.

Gerald Klerman, M.D.
Administrator, Alcohol, Drug Abuse, and Mental Health Administration
U.S. Department of Health and Human Services

FOREWORD

Natural disasters have been profoundly distressing to affected populations since ancient times. Recorded instances of a major earthquake in Syria, in 526 A.D., took 250,000 lives, while another as recently as 1976 killed more than 655,000 people in Tangshan, China. The largest toll in loss of life was recorded in 1931, when floods and tidal waves from the Hwang-ho River in China apparently accounted for the deaths of 3.7 million persons. Although disasters in other parts of the world have resulted in a greater loss of life than those in this country, major disasters continue to wreak havoc throughout the United States annually. Galveston, Texas, has the unenviable distinction of leading the nation in disaster-related fatalities; some 6,000 persons died there on September 8, 1900, due to a hurricane and related flooding.

In calender year 1979, there were forty-two major presidentially declared disasters in twenty-five states plus Puerto Rico, the Virgin Islands, and American Samoa. More than 38,000 families were housed apart from their home dwellings, while 207,449 families sought aid at disaster assistance centers. Total federal assistance in disasters exceeded the billion dollar mark at $1.3 billion; yet only $184,528 of this amount was spent for crisis counseling to treat debilitating emotional problems. Before the establishment of the Disaster Assistance and Emergency Mental Health Section at the National Institute of Mental Health, no money at all was spent for mental health disaster assistance services. Although line-item money is still unavailable for disaster research and training, service funds can be requested in presidentially declared disasters.

The number of lives lost does not always reflect the extent to which psychological problems may exist, since those who survive often experience numerous difficulties that leave turbulence and chaos in their wake. In Idaho, the Grand Teton Dam break in 1976 flooded a sizable portion of the state for eighty miles along the Snake River; yet only eleven persons lost their lives. The damage was so extensive, however, that one-stop service centers were established in six communities to provide relief to victims during the emergency phase of the disaster.

Crisis counseling services were supplied to more than a thousand persons. In 1978, as a result of severe storms and flooding in the Boston area, 84 persons died but 40,000 required food and assistance.

Curiously, despite the obvious damage to physical property, community disorganization and disruption, as well as loss of life, little attention has been given to the emotional or psychological aspects of disaster assistance, until the passage of the Disaster Relief Act of 1974, which included a section on crisis counseling. Prior to this, only a few professional articles were written on the subject. For example, in 1959, Glass discussed the psychological aspects of disaster and combat, and Popović and Petrović observed adverse psychological reactions after the Skoplje earthquake in Yugoslavia in 1963.

Paradoxically, although somewhat more attention is being given to the disaster assistance field, the problem is likely to get worse before it gets better. One reason for this is the fact that the geographic regions in the United States where disasters are most likely to occur are becoming the most heavily populated. Coastlines and river basin areas seem to attract people. The West Coast is particularly susceptible to earthquakes, landslides, fires, and floods. The East Coast and Gulf areas are regions frequently hit by tropical storms, hurricanes, and tornados. The Midwest and South have been particularly vulnerable to flooding and tornados. While the population explosion continues and we apparently become a more affluent society, there is an ever-increasing burden to be responsible for the welfare of our citizens, particularly in spheres where the victims are not blameworthy. In fact, this was the philosophical intent behind the Disaster Relief Act.

The earliest research dealing with the community problems in disaster emphasized such areas as floodplain management, mobility and rehousing problems, and issues of community organization. This work was carried out principally by non-mental health-oriented sociologists who believed it was important to discredit certain views about disaster held among the laity. Early workers felt there were a number of myths about behavioral reactions to disaster that should be dispelled. These workers did not observe panic reactions, widespread chaos and disruption, looting, or obvious mental disturbances, including anxiety, deep depressions, or psychoses. Instead, they believed, on the basis of a small number of short-term reactions, that persons behaved very responsibly and worked in a cohesive manner in every disaster situation. Recently, however, it has been documented in more than a dozen major disasters that victims do indeed experience marked emotional reactions and psychological distress in these situations. Common symptoms are psychophysiological disorders, anxiety, depression, sleep disturbances, anger, resentment, paranoid reactions, marital disturbances, alcoholism, and drug abuse. Moreover, there have been numerous instances of looting, with a breakdown in community cohesiveness and cooperation after the initial stages of the disaster.

How are communities to deal with these aspects of disaster? How can responsible administrators and mental health workers plan effectively and develop workable programs? What kinds of people are needed and how are they to be trained and prepared when disaster strikes? What kinds of intervention procedures seem most appropriate at different times during and after a disaster? How is a community to establish need for supplemental assistance in time of disaster? These questions are rudimentary, but they are invariably perplexing and create serious problems for disaster-stricken populations.

Drs. Cohen and Ahearn have performed a valuable service by writing this handbook. It will have value for administrative and organizational people, as well as for the practitioners of mental health services at various levels. The plain fact is that even most mental health professionals have not received up-to-date training in crisis intervention and emergency mental health work. This handbook appropriately introduces the reader to problems encountered in the various phases of disaster impact and sketches the problems that will be encountered. The basic concepts needed to understand disaster behavior are articulated by speaking of stress, crisis, loss, mourning, and grief, along with more unusual emotional responses.

The work is invaluable in helping personnel plan for an appropriate mental health service. It emphasizes the need to obtain sanction and the support of appropriate groups and individuals and describes how this can be done in the most effective manner. Education and consultation required for disaster work are delineated with clarity and skill. In discussing psychological intervention, the various time phases, ranging from the first few hours and days to problems encountered months later, are spelled out in detail. Real meaning is given to the work by citing actual experiences, such as those encountered in the Managua, Nicaragua, earthquake of 1972 and the severe storms and floods in the Boston area in 1978.

Awareness of and treatment for psychological problems in time of disaster will become more of a necessity as time goes on, for the issue has legal as well as humane ramifications. A judgment was found in favor of the plaintiffs in a class action suit against the Pittston Mining Company as the result of psychic impairment sustained when a dam broke and flooded the valley in Buffalo Creek, West Virginia, in February 1972. This judgment of $13.5 million established a legal precedent for such matters. So-called charitable immunity for nonprofit hospitals and governments is now being discarded more frequently, and it will behoove each locale to use this book to get its house in order, so to speak.

Perhaps the most commendable aspect of this work is its broad appeal.

It contains useful information for administrators and volunteers, for professional and nonprofessional workers alike. No matter how experienced or inexperienced readers of this book may be, they cannot help but find it a practical and stimulating effort. Every state mental health office and worker in the field of disaster assistance will do well to have a copy of this publication.

Calvin J. Frederick, Ph.D.
Chief, Disaster Assistance and Emergency Mental Health Section
National Institutes of Mental Health
U.S. Department of Health and Human Services

ACKNOWLEDGMENTS

Beginning with the 1970 Peruvian earthquake, then the earthquake in Managua, Nicaragua in 1972, the Johnstown, Pa., flood in 1978, and later the Massachusetts blizzard of 1978, the authors have had opportunities to observe human reactions under great stress. Our principal interest over these years became the intervention of mental health services to assist disaster victims. The distillation of our observations and experiences has led us to prepare, in a truly collaborative manner, this handbook for mental health practitioners and administrators. It is our hope that it will serve them as a guide if they must deal with the emotional after-effect of a catastrophe in their community.

We developed much of our conceptual thinking in Managua, where mental health personnel served more than 7,000 refugees. We are indebted to Dr. Berkley C. Hathorne and Dr. Ricardo Galbis, who had the vision of sending experts to Nicaragua for mental health assessment, planning, and intervention. Also, we appreciate the assistance of Dr. Simeón Rizo Castellón of Nicaragua, Drs. Claude de Ville de Goyet and René Gonzalez of the Pan American Health Organization, and Dr. Calvin Frederick of the National Institute of Mental Health for their support and review of our research into psychological consequences of disasters.

During the Massachusetts blizzard, we had an opportunity to try our ideas of mental health roles in shelters, hotels, and one-stop service centers in cooperation with our colleagues from the American Red Cross and the many relief agencies. Equally important was the opportunity to observe and exchange views with members of Project Concern, the federally assisted disaster project.

Finally, we acknowledge the hours of typing the many drafts of the manuscript by Mrs. Connie Heenan. The editorial assistance of Beverly Cronin and professional reviews by Drs. Carolyn Thomas and Thomas P. Hackett were helpful and appreciated.

1

DISASTERS AND MENTAL HEALTH

INTRODUCTION

The purpose of this handbook is to assist mental health administrators and practitioners in the design and implementation of effective services for disaster victims. The planning and provision of mental health care after a community disaster, whether natural or man-made, requires specific knowledge in a variety of areas. Major factors that affect the design and implementation of postdisaster mental health services include knowledge of the calamity and its consequences, knowledge of the disaster victims and their probable reactions, and knowledge of particular intervention methods for giving assistance. Most mental health administrators and workers have had little or no prior experience with catastrophes or their victims. When disaster strikes, there is an immediate need for knowledge and information before help can be planned or offered. Information about types of disasters and their consequences is necessary to provide a background of knowledge for developing specific relief efforts in the mental health area. From the disaster experiences of others, administrators and professionals must gain information about victims and their behavior. Finally, in order to plan and implement effective services, information is needed on the variety of mental health roles and techniques available for helping victims. This handbook offers mental health planners and workers some knowledge, information, and approaches toward providing mental health services after a disaster.

Disasters are not uncommon, but they are generally unexpected. Most communities are unprepared for the devastation and disorganization after an earthquake, flood, or tornado and thus are unable to respond quickly or effectively. Many residents of any given community cannot conceive that their town could be partially or totally destroyed by a calamity, yet this can and does happen. Mental health administrators and practitioners are similarly unprepared for such events.

Traditionally, the highest priorities in relief efforts have been the provision of food, shelter, and medical care. It is increasingly recognized, however, that psychological aid to victims in distress is also a priority. Thus it becomes obvious that preplanning and preparedness are as important in the area of mental health as they are for other relief activities. Mental health administrators need both knowledge and information in order to plan for mental health aid before a calamity occurs.

Any plan for mental health services following a disaster must include knowledge, information, assessment, and action. Knowledge of disaster-related psychological problems and information on how to resolve them can be obtained prior to a catastrophe. Once a disaster strikes, however, there is an urgent need for specific information and immediate assessment. Rapid action must be taken in the face of power loss and resulting telephone failures and difficulties in transportation. Communication problems contribute to a paucity of accurate information. During the early stages of a disaster it is hard to know what has happened, who and how many persons have been affected, where the psychological assistance is needed, and how to provide help. Ways to collect the needed information include contacts with media sources; in many cases, a personal, on-site visit to refugee shelters is required.

Once the general consequences of a disaster are known, a more complete assessment is required to detail specific groups of people who have suffered and to document the types of psychological problems being presented. Certain population groups may emerge as priority targets for services. The behavior of disaster victims varies over time and is interrelated with factors such as age, income level, previous mental health history, or degree of loss from the disaster. Finally, from the knowledge, information, and assessments available, a plan of action must be developed for mental health assistance to victims that reflects the realities of those impacted by the disaster and the type of behavioral and emotional problems they are experiencing.

Principal elements in the plan of action are the identification and selection of the various mental health roles to be implemented. Often these are innovative and flexible roles that differ in many respects from those usually employed in clinics or other mental health facilities. Practitioners working with disaster victims will encounter not only emotional stress, but stress related to day-to-day problems such as a need for shelter, income maintenance, medical care, locating missing relatives, or making arrangements for other services. Skills in crisis counseling and group treatment are required, as well as skills in outreach work, interagency referrals, community organization, and public education. Disaster victims seldom apply for service because the stigma of being labeled a mental patient is great among people in the "normal" population who suddenly find themselves in need of help. Therefore, mental health workers must actively search for those victims. This often means door-to-door searches in affected areas, or person-to-person referrals in emergency shelters. Any plan of action must recognize these factors, set forth the target groups for assistance, detail the scope and duration of the assistance project, and outline the interventive strategies to be employed.

In the event of a disaster, four major requirements must be addressed in developing a systematic plan for postdisaster mental health assistance. The first requirement is knowledge about disasters, disaster behavior, and interventive approaches. The second requirement is information as to what has happened and who has been affected. The third requirement is an assessment of the groups most impacted by loss and their associated psychological problems. The fourth requirement is a plan of action that details the goals, targets, strategies, duration, and scope of the proposed mental health project.

USES AND FORMAT OF THIS BOOK

This handbook provides information, procedures, and recommendations that have been developed to aid the mental health administrator and the professional in planning and implementing services to disaster victims. In this book mental health personnel will find essential information about:
- The types and the phases of a disaster;
- The concepts surrounding disaster-related behavior;
- Some specific physical and emotional problems suffered by disaster victims; and
- Some appropriate helping techniques to treat disaster victims.

This information may be useful in a variety of ways. For example, mental health administrators who live in disaster-prone areas may wish to do some predisaster planning. In order to have personnel prepared to go into action immediately after a catastrophe has occurred, service delivery strategies and staff development must be considered and disaster training programs designed for the professional staff. This book would be useful in designing such predisaster training.

After a disaster has struck an area, administrators will quickly need to identify the affected population, train their staffs, design specific service programs, and coordinate their efforts with others. At this time, mental health professionals must also be aware of the need to document what happens to disaster victims. The types of psychological symptoms presented and the range of service strategies that are effective in helping victims must be considered from the beginning and incorporated into the design of an information system that will permit an accurate evaluation of the program's efforts and will result in the reporting of results and findings to others.

Students of psychiatry, social work, psychology, nursing, and counseling will find this text useful in acquiring knowledge about disasters, about the behavior of disaster victims, and about methods that mental health practitioners can use to help those who have suffered as a result of a natural disaster.

The chapters of this book contain two broad sections: chapters 2 through 5 deal with mental health factors surrounding a disastrous event, and chapters 6 through 9 deal with mental health practices to assist victims of catastrophes.

Chapter 2 defines and examines the key concepts of (1) crisis and stress; (2) loss, mourning, and grieving; (3) social and emotional resources; and (4) coping and adaptation. These concepts are drawn from various studies of psychology and behavior and are seen as the basic tools of disaster knowledge. These concepts are later portrayed in two models of disaster behavior.

Chapter 3 extensively reviews the available disaster-related literature as a means to assess the types of symptoms and problems that victims present after a catastrophe. Although the assumption that subjection to natural hazards produces psychological consequences is still controversial in some circles, there is a growing body of knowledge to sustain this view. Chapter 3 also introduces models of disaster behavior that summarize the key concepts of the previous chapters and draw heavily from the literature.

Chapter 4 discusses many of the issues in planning and implementing a program of mental health services for individuals and families following a catastrophe. It suggests methods of approach to assess postdisaster needs, survey community resources, prepare a program, seek funding, and implement the program.

Chapter 5, recognizing the requirements of certain mental health roles, addresses the design of training programs and also reviews the activities required of the professional who serves as consultant and educator. This chapter includes various strategies to gain program support and to educate and report to the public through use of the media. It also describes techniques used by mental health practitioners to assist other relief and human service workers following a disaster.

Chapters 6 through 9 present specific suggestions and techniques for mental health practice under a variety of disaster situations. These chapters are divided by time phases after the calamity; they review the knowledge requirements, settings, roles, and techniques for each phase.

This book provides the mental health administrator and practitioner with a solid knowledge base for understanding how people react after a disaster and with a guide to practice in the first hours, days, and months of the calamity.

The reader may use this book under a variety of circumstances and for a variety of purposes. It is hoped that the flexibility designed into this work will provide access to disaster information and will prove useful to those who must provide or plan for mental health services in the event of disaster.

A DEFINITION OF DISASTER

Disasters are extraordinary events that cause great destruction of property and may result in death, physical injury, and human suffering. These events may be man-made or natural. Included in the first category are fires, war, civil disorder, terrorism, and chemical pollution, whereas floods, earthquakes, tidal waves, tornados, or hurricanes are natural calamities. The two categories have similarities in terms of potential mental health consequences, but the authors of this handbook, reflecting their experiences, focus primarily on disasters as acts of nature.

Catastrophes are usually unexpected but inevitable events that have a variety of characteristics. Some are slow in developing, while others occur suddenly and without any warning. Some wreak havoc over a wide area, while others are very site specific. These hazardous events also vary in their duration: Some persist for hours while others last only seconds or minutes. Finally, each disaster produces varying degrees of physical and human destruction. In unpopulated areas, an earthquake may cause little damage or harm, but in a densely populated area physical and human destruction may be great.

Disasters have been defined in many ways. Each of the following definitions emphasizes somewhat different outcomes of natural mishaps.

Harshbarger (1974) defines disasters as rapid and dramatic events that result in substantial damage and great harm. He stresses the importance of community life and postulates that disasters must be considered with reference to their potential to disrupt a community's activities and cause harm to its residents.

Erikson (1976) states that two different types of trauma, individual and collective, are evidenced in the behavior of persons affected by a disaster. He defines individual trauma as "a blow to the psyche that breaks through one's defenses so suddenly and with such force that one cannot respond effectively" and collective trauma as "a blow to the tissues of social life that damages the bonds linking people together and impairs the prevailing sense of community." Although one of these traumas can occur in the absence of the other, they are clearly inter-related, as they usually occur jointly and are experienced as two halves of a continuous whole in most large-scale disasters.

Schulberg (1974) discusses the link between risk events and personal reactions, using the concept of crisis. This concept has been explained in various ways, including a situation produced by one's environment, an individual's perception of an event, a clinical syndrome, the interaction of person and environment, and a critical change in role. Five features that distinguish crisis and are central to most viewpoints on crisis theory include:

- A time sequence that unfolds speedily;
- Major changes in behavior;
- Personal sense of helplessness;
- Tension within one's personal and social system; and
- Perception of personal threat.

Referring to disasters as crisis, Frederick (1977) is quick to distinguish between the terms "crisis" and "emergency." A crisis is a crucial period of time, varying from minutes to months, in which a situation affects a person's social or emotional equilibrium. As this evolves, it may develop into an emergency—a situation that presents an urgent demand and requires prompt action.

Anderson (1968) takes a different approach and defines disaster in terms of the affected population's reaction to the threat of a disaster before the disaster occurs. He describes the disaster as acute or chronic depending upon how a community responds to the threat. "Conceptually it is convenient to distinguish disaster as an *event* of acute crisis which physically disrupts otherwise 'normal' day-to-day life and causes palpable loss, from threat as a *situation* of chronic crisis which anticipates disruption in expected routine." He states that a disaster has different consequences for an individual, a family, and the various institutions of a stricken society. An acute crisis is one where the community lacks the established disaster-culture patterns that would allow it to deal with the unexpected events of a disaster. The community is caught completely by surprise. In a chronic crisis the events of the disaster are not completely unknown before the disaster occurs; the potential for threat is generally recognized before it is experienced by an individual.

Barton (1970) categorizes disasters as part of the larger group of collective stress situations that occur when many members of a social system fail to receive the expected conditions of life from the system. He adds that this collective stress can come from sources either outside or inside the system. Barton views the social system as a collectivity of human beings whose interaction maintains itself in identifiable patterns over a relatively long period of time; he states that systemic disequilibrium results from the stress of catastrophic events.

Barton says that the following factors must be considered in assessing these stress situations:

- The total scope of the situation (for instance, a small part of a system can be under stress either because it alone has suffered some major loss of input or because it is part of a larger system that is suffering such loss);

- The speed of onset;
- The duration of the stress agent (for instance, changes without warning are likely to create greater loss and leave the system with less capacity to respond than changes that give warning and allow preparation); and
- Social preparedness.

Kastenbaum (1974) describes a disaster in terms of the relative serious-ness of the mishap as compared with other major events. The way a person perceives a calamity has some relationship to the way one usually defines and classifies other events. The definition that something is a disaster requires a background of stability and normality with which the mishap is compared. It is thus recognized and finally identified as a disastrous event.

Traditionally, the study of disasters has emphasized the three phases of these events: preimpact, impact, and postimpact.

Preimpact Phase

This phase includes activities that precede the disaster itself, including threat and warning. A threat is the pervasive, long-term jeopardy pre-sented by possible calamity that places certain areas and inhabitants in greater risk than others. An example might be the threat to Californians who live along the San Andreas fault or the threat to residents of central Michigan who are exposed to the possibility of an earthquake or tor-nados. A warning may be vague and general, such as a flood alert, or specific, such as an immediate evacuation order. Interestingly, and usually unfortunately, threat and warning are routinely ignored by the populace. Some people have a fear of acting precipitously and appearing foolish. Others refuse to heed a threat or warning as a defense against something they wish would not happen. For example:

> Not everyone in the small mining town of Buffalo Creek Hollow, West Virginia, was sleeping soundly that disastrous night. Some of the coal miners had been around for many years, and they knew that the makeshift dam nearby could never hold the amount of water that lay behind it. Those who knew the danger of the mounting pressures had safely evacuated their families from the dangerous area. But others didn't know about the crumbling dam, and others just didn't believe the warnings. Those who didn't know or didn't believe were among the dead as 135 million gallons of water broke through the coal waste refuse dam with a deadly surge and roared down the valley. The force of the water, mixed with what the miners call gob—coal refuse—lifted houses off foundations, tore up railroad tracks, and sent scores of people swirling and flying to their death. Explosions rocked the valley as the force of the water stormed the power houses. One hundred and twenty-five people were dead, 1,000 homes were destroyed, and the area suffered over $50 million worth of damage before the water stopped its seventeen-mile, three-hour journey that morning on February 26, 1972.

Impact Phase

This phase is the period in which a community is struck by a hazard and the time afterward when the relief effort is organized. Researchers have indicated that during this phase, fear is the dominant emotion as victims seek safety for themselves and their families. Panic is unusual and only occurs when escape is impossible. Activities shortly after the disaster have been noted as part of the "heroic phase," when victims may act heroically to save themselves and others and when altruism is usually demonstrated. The first relief efforts are frequently begun by the victims who act to help their neighbors and other victims. Some authors use the term "rescue" to describe some of these relief activities, as well as the term "inventory" to refer to the assessment of physical and human damage. Following is an example of the first stage of this phase:

> After the San Francisco earthquake in 1906, news reports around the country featured headlines such as "Little Left of Frisco; Thousands Homeless," "Parks Are Full of Sufferers," "Made A Noise Like Dynamite," "The Earth Moved Visibly," and "Crockery was Smashed, Clocks Were Stopped, Houses Tottered and Hundreds Dead." Our worst and most legendary disaster caused the death of 700 persons. Jack London, the noted writer, reported his eyewitness account in *Collier's Weekly*, May 5, 1906: "On Wednesday morning at quarter past five came the earthquake. A minute later the flames were leaping upward. In a dozen different quarters south of Market Street, in the working-class ghetto, and in the factories, fires started. There was no opposing the flames. There was no organization, no communication. All the shrewd contrivances and safeguards of man had been thrown out of gear by thirty seconds' twitching of the earthcrust" (Gelman and Jackson, 1976).

Postimpact Phase

This phase begins several weeks after the disaster has struck and usually includes the continued activities of relief, as well as the assessment of types of problems that individuals may experience. Elements of this phase have been called "remedy and recover"; they include the actions taken to ameliorate the situation and to facilitate individual and familial recovery. Some writers have referred to two additional elements of the postimpact phase—"honeymoon" and "disillusionment." The honeymoon is the period of time shortly after the disaster and up to several months later, when victims demonstrate considerable energy in reconstructing their lives. During the honeymoon there is a need to ventilate feelings and to share experiences with others. Considerable organized support is offered victims at this time to help them cope with their problems. "Disillusionment" sets in when this organized support is withdrawn, or when the victims face considerable red tape in resolving their problems, or when it becomes obvious that their lives have been permanently changed.

The postimpact phase may continue for the rest of the victim's life. New problems may arise from the social disorganization caused by the disaster. Erikson (1976) has referred to this as "the second disaster." After the Buffalo Creek flood in West Virginia, many victims were relocated to trailer camps, where some began to express psychological reactions to their new living arrangements and to the lack of friendship with their new neighbors. Long-term personal problems characterized by apathy, depression, and chronic anxiety have been called "the disaster syndrome." Finally, a few writers have addressed the "reconstruction element" of the postdisaster phase, when the victims have begun to resolve their problems and the destroyed areas are rebuilt. This process may take several years.

A DEFINITION OF DISASTER VICTIMS

The term "victim" in this book refers to those individuals and families who have suffered from the disaster or its consequences. Disaster victims have experienced an unexpected and stressful event. It is widely assumed that most victims have been functioning adequately before the catastrophe, but that their ability to cope may have been impaired by the stresses of the situation. Even though victims may present symptoms of physical or psychological stress, they do not view themselves as experiencing pathology. Disaster victims may include all ages, socioeconomic classes, and racial or ethnic groups because catastrophes affect the entire cross-section of the population in an impacted area.

Some victims may suffer more than others, depending upon several interrelated factors. Those who may be particularly susceptible to physical and psychological reactions from a disaster include people who:
- Are vulnerable from previous traumatic life events;
- Are at risk due to recent ill health;
- Experience severe stress and loss;
- Lose their system of social and psychological supports; and
- Lack coping skills.

The elderly are a group that, in general, may find it difficult to cope with disasters and their consequences. It is not unusual to find older victims who are isolated from their support systems and live alone. As a result, they are often afraid to seek help. Typical postcatastrophe problems with this group are depression and a sense of hopelessness. Unfortunately, a common response among some elderly people is a lack of interest in rebuilding their lives.

Children are also a special group because they usually do not have the capacity to understand and rationalize what has happened. Consequently, they may present emotional or behavioral problems at home or school. Perhaps the most prominent disturbances reported after disasters have been phobias, sleep disturbances, loss of interest in school, and difficult behavior.

Those with a history of mental illness may require special attention. Under the stress of a disaster situation, relapses often occur in this population due to the additional stress burden or the difficulties in obtaining regular medication.

Finally, another at-risk group to be considered by the mental health disaster worker includes those who, at the time of the disaster, were experiencing certain life crises. Members of this group might include, for example, people who have recently been widowed or divorced and those who have recently undergone major surgery. These victims may display a special vulnerability to the stresses generated by a natural disaster.

In summation, although the particular at-risk groups identified merit close attention from the disaster worker, victims can be found among all social, economic, and ethnic strata and among all segments of the population in the disaster area.

A DEFINITION OF MENTAL HEALTH
ADMINISTRATORS AND PRACTITIONERS

The titles assumed by mental health administrators differ from place to place and include such terms as medical director, program administrator, commissioner, clinic director, or superintendent. The term administrator, as used in this book, encompasses all of these titles and denotes the specific person or persons with the authority and responsibility to carry out mental health policy and program goals and to design projects. This book is written for and directed to those administrators who would be responsible for planning a program of psychological assistance for disaster victims.

In this book, the terms mental health practitioner, worker, and professional are used synonymously. These individuals include psychiatrists, social workers, psychologists, community organizers, psychiatric nurses, and counselors. If they have not had specific disaster experiences, they should receive orientation, training, and supervision. Presumably these professionals, through knowing about disasters, understanding the unique situation of each victim, and anticipating the possible behavioral adaptations to a catastrophe, will be able to assist individuals and families following a disastrous event.

This book is not specifically written for nonprofessionals or paraprofessionals, although they are an integral part of the mental health team in disasters. Paraprofessionals such as community workers, psychiatric assistants, and volunteers often do outreach work, give support to victims, help them get to and obtain other services, and interpret services to the community. To assist paraprofessionals in these kinds of activities, professionals may wish to use this handbook to design training and orientation programs.

2

GENERAL CONCEPTS IN UNDERSTANDING DISASTER BEHAVIOR

This chapter presents a number of key concepts considered fundamental to the understanding of how disaster victims react. Most mental health practitioners already know and use these concepts in their practice, but the authors believe these concepts are also basic to the development of theories that explain behavior after catastrophes. As these concepts and theories are identified and described in this handbook, professionals may gain a better understanding of which range of reactions are common, and they may be able better to diagnose and treat victims suffering from reactive emotional impairment.

This foundation knowledge includes these key interrelated concepts:
- Stress and crisis;
- Loss, mourning, and grieving;
- Social and emotional resources; and
- Coping and adaptation.

Earthquakes, floods, or tornados are stressors that affect the psychophysiologic equilibrium of the victim, and the stress they produce may result in personal crisis. This crisis period is frequently a crucial turning point for the victim—one that influences both present and future emotional and behavioral reactions.

A catastrophe always causes varying types and degrees of personal loss resulting from death, injury, unemployment, or destruction of property. A victim who has suddenly lost an intimate, meaningful bond characterized by ambivalence will experience a process of grieving similar to what generally happens when a person sustains the natural death of a family member, meaningful relative, or close friend. In disasters, however, mental health practitioners should remember that this sense of loss and change may come not only from death, but also from the destruction of one's personal property and the devastation of one's environment. Frequently victims mourn the bond loss of the security and the familiarity of their home, their valued mementos, or their neighborhood. An individual also goes through a grieving process when loss of income is sustained either through destruction of property and/or unemployment.

A person's psychological and behavioral response to a disaster is conditioned by his/her system of social and emotional supports that help resolve stress reactions. The nature of a person's social matrix may also produce powerful influences to protect him or her from the aftermath of a crisis event. An individual's psychophysiologic mechanisms and internal resources, as well as the supportive network of family and friends, are extremely important in this process of readaptation and resolution. An addition to these personal resources might include assistance and services available in the community to help the person in distress.

Coping as an interrelated set of psychophysiologic mechanisms stimulated by stress and crisis, loss and mourning, and operant support systems, promotes types of behavior that are designed to achieve a state of equilibrium. These adaptive behaviors protect the individual by avoiding, altering, or managing the stresses of disaster.

These four concepts will be examined in this chapter so that mental health professionals can relate their knowledge about the dynamics of disaster with expected reactions, in order to facilitate their recognition and treatment of these problems.

STRESS AND CRISIS

Stress

Stress and crisis are interrelated psychophysiologic concepts. Stress consists of physical and emotional reactive tensions that can emanate from objective events and/or external stimuli, called stressors. A natural disaster unchains a series of stressors that cause varying levels of tensions for its victims. Theorists have associated stress with a variety of factors, which vary by source and by type as well as by the suggested mechanism for discomfort resolution. These factors include the following approaches:

- Antecedent, mediating, and intervening factors;
- Changes in one's biological-physiologic systems;
- Impact and perception variations on a person's cognitive process; and
- Stressors as social and psychological events and their symbolic meaning.

One author defines stress as those internal forces that resist external threats, and links this concept with the body's response to symbolic experiences and social and psychological events. Stress, then, is the interactive force between the body's organism and one's external environment (Wolff, 1953). Another author defines stress as a state manifested by specific symptoms consisting of changes within the biological system that have been induced by a group of stimuli or agents (stressors). Using the notion of homeostasis as a regulatory system within the body, he states that the stress condition is an outcome for self-preservation when one is attacked by these external agents (Seyle, 1956). Lazarus also employs the theory of equilibrium and sees stress as related to cognitive processes when one faces threat and must appraise what has happened. When an individual anticipates psychological or physical harm, levels of stress increase and may immobilize the individual or cause feelings of hopelessness expressed as anxiety (Lazarus, 1974).

In addition, researchers have described stress as the outcome of disrupting customary activities; the source of that disruption may be antecedent, mediating, or intervening factors. Acting to increase or decrease stress, these factors consist of prior events (stressors) that have not been fully resolved, internal and external constraints, affective cognitive processes, and one's social expectations (Dohrenwend and Dohrenwend, 1978).

New findings of substances called endorphins may help clarify stress reactions. This group of brain chemicals composed of protein molecules may be a key factor in the brain's system to signal and register emotional behavior. These molecules are potent, specific, and selective in their actions on nerve cells and appear to be linked to certain aspects of behavior. The endorphins are believed to act as transmitters of signals between nerve cells. The true functions of the endorphins and the regions of the brain in which they function are still unknown, but their structural relation to pain and to the neural pathways of emotions offers a hypothetical construct that can be linked to stress behavior through physiological modulation of behavior, pain perception, and emotional regulation (Snyder, 1978).

To summarize:

- Stress is envisioned as a state within the total organism of the individual and can be related, at a specific point in time, to a person's psychophysical condition;
- A variety of environmental stimuli can produce stress;
- Individuals respond differently to the same stimuli. Some appear immune to stimuli stressors while others are particularly vulnerable to conditions that produce personal disequilibrium;
- Stress states produce psychobiological responses of varying lengths. These responses will be determined by the number, frequency, intensity, duration, and priority of the demands made on the coping system of the individual; and
- Reactions vary depending upon the context, the force of the stressor, the state of the individual's health, the types of support

systems in the community, the family network, and the individual's habitual patterns of human interaction. In general, the stress system may be viewed as fluctuating, open-ended, dynamic, and fluid.

The situation of Mr. M., a 38-year-old salesman who lost his wife and only child in a major midwestern flood, exemplifies a stress reaction to loss of loved ones, home, and job:

> Mr. M. was interviewed on the fourth day after the disaster. He had objected to some routine questioning to itemize the objects he had lost, with the objective of replacing them. When faced with focusing on the concrete task of describing the objects, he broke down and started to cry. He composed himself in a few minutes, excused himself, and tried to explain how "strange" it was for him to feel tense and frightened all the time. He related this condition directly to the time he became aware of the flooding waters and to the consequences that followed. He described difficulty in swallowing and feelings of dread whenever anyone approached him. He could not concentrate enough to understand what people asked him. Instead, he became aware of his heart "racing" and his stomach contracting, and he experienced heightened feelings of irritability. He felt he could not stand another demand or intrusion into his life and wanted to be left alone. Everything was too much of an effort for him. He believed the "bureaucrats" were efficient but cold and insensitive and that they added to his stress.

Crisis

A crisis is a crucial period in a person's life, a turning point that has both physical and emotional consequences. Specifically, a crisis is a time-limited period of psychological disequilibrium, precipitated by a sudden and significant change in an individual's life situation. This change results in demands for internal adjustments and the use of external adaptation mechanisms that are temporarily beyond the individual's capacity.

The individual in crisis may be seen as a holistic system, affected by an interplay of dynamic changes. These changes occur when forces of different levels of strength collide. These forces in turn are continuously influenced by natural, occurring, regulatory bio-psychic mechanisms designed to bring about a state of balance and personal equilibrium. There are both inputs and outputs of energy and information into the system. The essential point of crisis is that the intensity of a system's energy exceeds the capacity of the organism to adjust and adapt. The individual is overwhelmed and the system goes into a state of disequilibrium or imbalance.

The severe fluctuation of individual homeostasis in the face of a crisis event is produced by the disorganization of psychological and somatic systems. The consequences of this fluctuation include severe personal tension and stress. This imbalance may be induced by the death of a loved one, loss of income or property, illness, divorce, birth, relocation, or other important personal factors. As an outcome, changes in role patterns and in usual or expected behaviors often produce, as a secondary consequence, problems of interpersonal relationships. As these changes present themselves, the individual tends to develop new patterns and behaviors in order to manage stress and therefore diminish discomfort and pain.

An example of a precipitous change in life situation is highlighted by the following story told during a recovery effort after a hurricane:

> A 48-year-old mother of two adolescents, recently divorced, was trapped in her car by fallen electric wires. She had to remain under that danger for over seven hours until the rescuing team extricated her. She was brought to a shelter, where she found out that her neighborhood had been severely damaged. No one, however, could inform her as to whether her two children were safe, nor to which shelter they had been taken. For three days she tried to find out, but due to road conditions, disrupted phone lines, and the other priorities of the few disaster workers, she was unable to get information. When interviewed, she expressed anxiety and shocked feelings at how she was being "pushed around." Her speech was rambling, repeating over and over how she should never have left her children alone. She already felt that the divorce had been traumatic enough to them and now, again, she felt that she was a bad mother. Her sense of helplessness, anguish, disorientation, self-accusations, and continuous and frantic attempts to find out where her children were, coupled with her refusal to listen to or accept any explanations, reflect the first cycle of crisis behavior.

The crisis model has considerable significance for mental health workers helping disaster victims. First, it conveys an understanding that certain life events produce a loss of habitual modes of behavior due to the personal turmoil, tension, and emotional upset that accompany stress. Second, the theory of crisis situations signals crucial periods when an individual is faced with ongoing decisions that have long-term implications for subsequent life styles and levels of adjustment.

One example of a crucial period is the bereavement following an important loss. To understand the role of bereavement, the quality of the personal relations that have been severed should be examined. A high percentage of mourners cannot move beyond the hopeless, giving-up stage. This in turn precipitates different levels of depression, including interference with all the decision-making functions necessary for victims to reorganize their lives. Because of this inability to deal with all the human and bureaucratic interactions necessary to obtain relief resources, the crisis feelings intensify. The continuation and intensification of the individual's apprehension of the crisis situation stimulates a circular down-spiral leading to and including a lack of energy, depression, passivity, loss of self-esteem, and helpless behavior. The way an individual deals with a problem during a period of emotional stress influences whether one emerges from crisis with increased susceptibility to mental disorder or an increased likelihood of improved coping capacity.

Third, crisis theory shows that the individual in a state of disequilibrium expresses two parallel characteristics, one of hope and reaching out for help, the other increased susceptibility to influence by outside forces. Given these two characteristics, it is a propitious time for mental health intervention.

Crisis, then, is a life situation that involves change, threat, or challenge resulting in personal imbalance or disequilibrium. It may emanate from developmental factors such as puberty, pregnancy, or middle age, or from accidental factors such as a car crash, fire, or natural disaster.

Other points in crisis theory:

- The objective reality of a crisis is the expression of societal norms, values, and culture and therefore will differ depending upon the people or society involved. Some groups will define a certain event as producing crisis while others will not;
- The process of subjective interpretation of a hazardous event modifies what society has objectively defined. Individuals will give different meaning to the event, depending on their perception of what has occurred, their past experience with hazardous events, and their success or lack of success in managing its impact; and
- The process of reconstitution involves marshaling personal and social resources in the search for equilibrium and effective functioning. During this final phase emerges individual activation of the skills necessary to cope. By coping, one may attempt to change, reduce, or modify a problem; one may devalue an event by seeking satisfaction elsewhere; or one may become resigned to what has happened and then attempt to manage the resulting stress. This final phase of crisis involves finding appropriate defenses and ways to master negative feelings during this state of turmoil.

Finally, it should be added that stress and crisis are concepts associated with loss and mourning, social and emotional supports, and coping and adaptation. It is evident that a calamity such as a fire, hurricane, or earthquake is a hazardous event that produces stress and crisis. The phases of crisis and its psychological dimensions are of extreme importance to mental health workers attempting to understand disaster victims and to intervene in offering them psychological help.

LOSS, MOURNING, AND GRIEVING

Another set of concepts that is of particular use in disaster work consists of loss, mourning, and grieving. The last two terms almost always refer to the reaction produced by loss, especially the death of an important individual in a person's emotional life. Although the discussion of loss usually focuses upon death, it may include property destruction or sudden unemployment; impaired physical, social, or psychological function; or separation. Mourning and grieving, then, are emotional processes that emanate from an experience of loss, and it follows that disaster victims may experience a process of mourning and grieving.

Among many other professionals, Kübler-Ross has been calling attention to the processes of death and dying. Individuals faced with the imminence of their own death or of persons close to them go through a five-stage process: denial, rage and anger, bargaining, depression, and acceptance (Kübler-Ross, 1976). It has been said that these five stages do not always occur or do not always appear in a specific order, but the stages and their order are strongly influenced by the person's total personality and philosophy of life (Shneidman, 1976).

The processes of mourning and grieving, sometimes called bereavement, involve cognitive elements and are frequently expressed by physical and psychological symptoms. The process begins with recognition and acceptance of the loss. The individual needs to come to grips with reality in not only intellectual but also emotional terms. When only an intellectual acceptance of loss occurs, the chance of emotional maladaptation increases. The process of grieving takes a person from shock through acute distress to resignation. Along the way the individual may suffer physical discomfort or increased susceptibility to illness, may withdraw into apathy, may express increased hostility toward others, or may become totally isolated (Lindemann, 1944).

The description of the bereavement behavior of victims after the Coconut Grove nightclub fire in Boston in 1942 shows many aspects of behavior found in shelters and temporary housing after a disaster involving severe loss. For instance, a predominant reaction is a strong defense of denial—that is, victims appear to be preoccupied with activities or conversations that do not include mentioning the loss. This delayed reaction appears to facilitate coping with uncontrollable emotions. Another example is as follows:

The behavior of Mrs. S., a 29-year-old woman who lost her fiancé one month before their marriage exemplifies the delayed reaction defense. An earthquake had toppled a roof and killed her future husband. The victim became the assistant to the head nurse at the disaster shelter and busily kept the pharmacy in order. She moved bottles and pill containers from one shelf to another, sorted all first-aid materials, and made long lists of items on hand or needing replacement. Any reference to her fiancé would make her turn her face away and change the conversation; no emotional sign of her stress or sadness was expressed. However, three weeks later she was seen at a crisis center, depressed and agitated. She had lost weight, was unable to sleep, and showed signs of mild paranoid ideation. With counseling help she was able to begin to acknowledge her loss, her ambivalent feelings for her fiancé, and her anger about the experience.

Another author, Peter Marris, has described these processes in a slightly different way. He sees mourning as the societal expression of bereavement that is usually articulated in religious practice or ritual. Grief is described as the feeling of profound conflict between contradictory impulses: to conserve all that is valuable and important from the past and at the same time to commence life anew, accepting the loss that has been sustained. If the grieving process is cut short in the search for immediate readjustment and reintegration, or if it is continued endlessly in preoccupation for what has been lost, the bereaved may never recover emotionally. Grief is mastered by abstracting what has been fundamentally important in the lost person or object and then facing life and accepting the new reality (Marris, 1975).

It is generally agreed that grieving is a process that begins with sadness, fear, anxiety, and anger, proceeds through pain and despair, and usually ends with renewed confidence and hope. These phases express the urge to recover the lost bond-person or object, they involve personal disorganization and emotional upsets, and they conclude with reorganization and adaptation (Bowlby, 1961). When an intimate bonded person is lost, the nature, severity, and outcome of the grieving process will depend upon many factors. These include the past relationship with the person lost; the mourner's personality, state of health, and age; and one's social and economic situation at the moment of grieving (Gut, 1974).

As indicated earlier, mourning and grieving can be associated with losses other than those due to death. A sense of loss may also derive from an inability to achieve goals or to attain valued freedom or independence. The resulting feelings of disappointment, deprivation, or failure generate dynamic forces with powerful consequences. These may contibute to pathological states and affect one's achievements. In this sense, loss also involves some form of mourning or grief. For example, an elderly person may experience a profound sense of loss from a slowing of physical functioning associated with age (Rochlin, 1965).

Sudden loss due to dislocation or relocation of families may also produce a process of grieving and increased anxiety. One author noted that a slum clearance project in Nigeria caused families to feel that they had lost the familiar surroundings of their neighborhoods and the social relationships developed over the years. Grief was a common reaction for these people (Marris, 1975). Fried had made a similar finding in Boston, where a dislocated Italian population grieved over the loss of their homes, neighborhoods, and social attachments. As the familiarity and structure of attachments are seldom reestablished in a new and alien setting, relocated persons demonstrate a variety of symptoms including anger, a sense of helplessness, somatic distress, and a tendency to idealize one's former home (Fried, 1963).

It is logical to assume that all disaster victims experience varying degrees of loss. The most serious, of course, is the loss of a loved one. The mourning and grieving over this loss is complicated by the chaotic aftermath, which may include additional loss due to property destruction, relocation, and unemployment. Many disasters do not cause large numbers of deaths, but they may rob victims of home, mementos, neighborhood, and income. In these cases, it can be expected that disaster victims may experience a profound sense of loss, producing a mourning and grieving process. This is aggravated by the looting and vandalism that may follow a disaster.

SOCIAL AND EMOTIONAL RESOURCES

The social and emotional resources of the disaster victim are related to the victim's experience of stress and crisis, of loss and mourning, of coping and adaptation. What is usually referred to as a person's emotional and social support network will greatly influence an effective outcome to a disaster experience. For this reason, the mental health practitioner must be keenly aware of the types of social and emotional resources refugees have at their disposal, in order to assist them by linking and reinforcing this social matrix and therefore increasing their potentiality to cope with disaster stress. Traditional, stable, and structured social groups tend to promote strong bonds and thus help protect their members against postcrisis pathological outcomes.

An individual's resources are found within his emotional capacity, which is integrated within his social network. This is a fluctuating situation, with increased crisis potential as the age of the individual advances. *Emotional resources* are a group of genetic and physiologic endowments that includes the psychological skill and capacities of an individual, usually based upon past experience, which he uses to deal with the stress of a problem in order to resolve it. These emotional resources enable the person to withstand the pressures of stress, anxiety, and depressive feelings and to have the confidence that helps clearly define reality for the purpose of setting goals and taking effective action. When these resources are not enough to withstand the tension, the individual frequently succumbs to stress and expresses nonadaptive behaviors. *Social resources* are the sum total of an individual's relations; they form a network of social linkages or interrelationships with individuals and groups for the purpose of defining and gaining emotional reassurance (Tolsdorf, 1976; Caplan, 1974).

In dealing with a stressful event, an individual usually first calls upon his reserve of internal emotional mechanisms in order to resolve the problem at hand. When personal mobilization fails, an individual then uses the supports of his social network. This coping strategy, relying first on personal and then on social resources, is the generalized pattern for most individuals. Persons with mental illness, however, will often tend to rely first on social resources. If they fail, they employ their own emotional capacities (Speck and Rueveni, 1969).

It has been found that the quality of one's social network and the sociocultural context of the individual when acting within it are significant determinants of coping behavior. The social network may be a major force in maintaining certain forms of behavior or may be an important factor in determining the degree and direction of change. In either case, the network of relationships may provide the support to change or not to change, and may facilitate efforts to adapt or not to adapt, based upon the social and cultural values of the situation (Hammer, 1963).

The social network or support system has also been defined as that group of individuals who influence each other's lives by fulfilling specific human needs. For the individual, this is the fountain of love, affection, respect, approval, and self-definition. The linkages in a social network of supports depend upon the type and quality of communication among members. Thus, in employing this concept in treatment efforts, the mental health practitioner should seek to:

- Create a climate of openness and trust among network members;
- Facilitate interrelationships between system actors;
- Examine a person's behavior vis á vis the support system by focusing upon ways to modify or change it if necessary; and
- Make required changes in the social network by altering interrelationships between its members (Speck, 1969).

In times of stress, individuals may use both formal and informal support systems to help them manage their problems. An example in the use of *formal supports* is the case of workers in a mental health facility who, suffering from severe job pressures, decided to improve formally the channels of communication among themselves. This was done by initiating regular group meetings designed to enhance the expression of feeling, the sharing of support, and the giving of advice and feedback in order to enable workers to cope more effectively with their job tensions (Pines and Maslack, 1978).

An example of *informal supports* is given by Gottlieb (1975) in his research on high school adolescents. Dividing his sample into four groups (elites, isolates, deviants, and outsiders), he analyzed how each group coped with social, family, and educational problems. He found that when informal helpers (employers, teachers, clergyman, neighbors, or relatives) were available during the early stages of a problem and were accepted during the problem-solving process, adolescents used these helpers as their first line of defense against the loss of social and emotional equilibrium.

Group affiliation as a means of developing one's social support network is necessary when individuals have been displaced or relocated, or have suffered severe isolation. In studying survivors of Nazi concentration camps, one author found that an inmate's ability to cope was directly associated with the creation of support systems through group affiliations. It was this network that provided the inmate with information, advice, protection, and reinforcement of individuality and worth. For those who failed to affiliate in the first days of internment, chances of survival became increasingly limited (Dimsdale, 1974).

Although there is not an extensive body of literature that specifically addresses the need and use of social support systems during and after a major disaster, a few studies have been conducted in this area. In one analysis of disaster victims, successful coping was directly related to the use of one's support system. Immediately after a calamity, individuals who relied primarily on their linkages to relatives and close friends and less so upon neighbors and formal or voluntary organizations generally were able to deal effectively with the stresses of the catastrophe. Even three years later, these disaster victims had stronger ties to their social support system than before the catastrophe (Drabek and Key, 1976). Family and friends are the most important sources of psychological skepticism about the utility of most formal helping organizations. This holds true regardless of socioeconomic status (Erikson, Drabek, Key, and Crowe, 1976).

Disaster victims have frequently been relocated to trailer parks (refugee camps) without regard for the natural support network of individuals and families. Many social and emotional problems that arise in these camps have been associated with the unfamiliarity and suspicion of the new environment, as well as with the loss of the social support network (Hall and Landreth, 1975). According to these authors, individuals and families will first call upon their emotional resources to manage the stress of their situations in the aftermath of a natural disaster and then will most likely need the psychological support of family and friends in order to cope with disaster-related stress.

Mental health professionals, therefore, must be alert to the existence and use of systems for social and emotional supports by disaster victims. Obviously, a person distressed by a major tragedy will turn to internal psychological resources and the support of family and friends and finally to the more structured and formal services provided by the community.

In sum, a variety of support systems aid the victim in coping with disaster stresses and in seeking personal adaptation.

COPING AND ADAPTATION

Another key interrelated concept toward understanding disaster behavior is that of coping and adaptation. This section will review the meaning of coping, the interrelationship of coping to stress and socio-emotional support systems, and the elements of coping behavior directed toward adaptation and health. Although there are many definitions of coping, we shall define it as *the behavior that protects the individual from internal and external stresses.* The behavior implies adaptation, defense, and mastery (White, 1974). Protection behavior usually takes three courses:

- Alteration of conditions producing stress;
- Redefining the meaning of the stress-producing experience so as to downgrade its significance; and
- Manipulating the emotional consequences· so as to place them within manageable bounds (Pearlin and Schooler, 1978).

Coping is the behavior designed to prevent, alter, avoid, or manage tension and stress and is employed by almost all individuals some of the time. It should not be interpreted as unusual or rare behavior. Most individuals learn ways to deal with stress, and although these vary, they usually follow the pattern of avoidance, alteration, management, prevention, or control of undue emotional stress.

Stress is always associated with crisis and is the emotional discomfort felt by individuals experiencing persistent problems or undue demands. It emanates from unusual, uncommon, or unexpected pressures—for example, the fear of undergoing surgery (Janis, 1958), the competition of doctoral study, and the impact of a natural disaster (Ahearn, 1976). Stress is associated with a particular event or situation and differs from anxiety or depression, which is more generalized and diffuse. Stress varies somewhat but is interrelated with strain, the result of everyday problems that may arouse concern. This usually emanates from conflicts in one's role, such as the strain of being a parent, working, being married, or relating socially. Coping is the behavioral response to stress and strain that serves to defend the individual from incapacitating emotional harm.

Coping is intertwined with one's social and emotional resources. It is helped and made easier, or hampered and prevented, by the nature of a person's social matrix, i.e., the network of interpersonal relationships with family, friends, neighbors, co-workers, and small group associations. It is to this social system that individuals turn first when seeking support, understanding, or aid in problem resolution. However, coping also depends upon one's emotional or psychological tools—those personal characteristics of individual strengths and weaknesses. These resources include one's ability to communicate, one's sense of self-esteem, and one's capacity for bearing discomfort without disorganization or despair. Communication skill facilitates expression of the problem and the means to seek help to resolve it. Self-esteem refers to one's positive feelings toward self; its absence would indicate low self-image. Emotional resources generally represent what people are, whereas coping refers to what people do to resolve stress.

Although coping usually incorporates behavioral responses for action, it also employs cognitive and perceptual actions as well. These coping actions may take three different directions. First, coping responses may attempt to change the source of strain or stress. This action presumes knowledge and perception of its causes. Attention is focused upon changing the situation (cause) before strain or stress occurs. In effect, this strategy is designed to avoid threat situations.

Second, coping responses may attempt to redefine the threat situation so as to control the degree of stress. This strategy is usually activated if one cannot control the course of stress or strain in order to lessen or buffer its impact on the individual. Redefinition is the way the meaning and gravity of the problem situation are managed. Again, cognition and perception are important in this process. This action is developed so that the individual may be able to say that the problem situation is not too important an area to be upset about. This may be done by making comparisons and then concluding that things could be worse. Or one may selectively ignore the negative aspects and emphasize the positive.

Third, coping responses may attempt to manage the stress of a problem situation so that the individual can continue to function as normally as possible. This action is essentially an effort to keep stress within controllable boundaries and is a help in bringing about an accommodation to stress without being overwhelmed by it. This third coping strategy involves a variety of responses, including denial, withdrawal, passive acceptance, undue optimism, avoidance, or even magical thinking.

The following case report represents an example of a disaster victim who was able to cope with many stress-inducing events following the loss of her home due to a dam break and the subsequent death of her husband after a heart attack. She seemed to manifest coping strategies that enabled her to manage her problems with minimal psychosomatic distress. Moreover, this victim spontaneously used coping methods that have been noticed in other victims.

Coping and defending are two categories of psychological adaptation processes that can appear simultaneously in the same individual. Whereas the victim described below used an active problem-solving approach in dealing with all the demands of the rescue and relief agencies, she was also able to defend herself by modulating and confronting reality in a way so that she avoided having to deal all at once with the enormity of her losses. By dealing with the disaster in segments, she was able to assimilate the new stressful events in which she found herself as she tried to obtain funding, find a new house, visit her husband in the hospital, and later attend to the funeral arrangements. She tried to accommodate herself to all the situations, and she used the support assistance offered by a crisis counselor. Her use of defenses were obvious, especially during the mourning process after the death of her husband.

Mrs. L., a 64-year-old widow, suffered from the incidents just described. She and her husband had retired five years earlier when both were laid off from work due to a business closure. Despite serious economic problems, they were able to pay the final mortgage on their house. Mrs. L. cared for her ailing husband during the last few years before his death. Several years before, her son had deserted his family, leaving Mrs. L. to raise two grandchildren. Later the son returned. He had lost his job in another city and needed both emotional and financial support. There were seldom enough funds, but Mrs. L. managed well by taking some babysitting jobs. She did not seek public assistance.

In the midst of trying to deal with the recovery agency operations following relocation to a temporary house, and during the terminal hospitalization of her husband, Mrs. L. developed intense headaches that were diagnosed as psychosomatic. She continued to meet regularly with the crisis counselor assigned to her, thus maintaining a support system for herself. Some of the material that she shared with the counselor revealed information and personal data pertaining to past occupation, family, religion, medical history, and so forth. During these meetings, Mrs. L. shared her philosophy and approach to solving problems. She appeared to belong to a group of victims that show low emotional distress. Because of the disparity between the seriousness of her losses, her age group, and the manifestation and quality of her emotional distress, she could be singled out as a victim who mobilized her coping abilities within each crisis situation. Some of her characteristics showed that Mrs. L. was clearly optimistic, not only expecting to solve her problem but hoping eventually to resolve her losses. Instead of feeling imposed upon by the paper work and inspections, she reported feeling good about the agency staff and the help from her counselor. She voiced some resentment about her plight and the possibility of negligence in the "check-up" of the dam, but was able to find satisfaction in whatever she was called upon to do. While fully realizing the serious implication of her losses, she was not fearful of the future, stating that her social problems could be managed, just as they had been in the past.

Mrs. L. Was essentially a private person who did not easily relinquish emotional control, nor did she confide in others. However, she was cooperative, cordial, and appreciative in a quiet way. Mrs. L. avoided excessive emotional expressions of all kinds, preferring to modulate responses and maintain personal control. She grasped all the agency approaches offered to help her with her problems. She showed an above-average memory, good social judgment, conceptual ability, and a good awareness of reality within the chaos of her present life.

Mrs. L. tended to use positive self-reinforcement. She asked appropriate questions and listened to options. She was able to use help to become aware of and assess the solutions available to her. This was a customary way in which she had always behaved prior to the disaster. She had a practical, common-sense orientation to life. Her cognitive style was also practical, and she tended to be more concrete than conceptual about her daily tasks. She preferred concrete details, viewing the environment as something that need not be actively shaped or modified. Her "take things as they come" attitude added to her flexible ways of looking at problems. This method of thinking appeared to control any emotions based on her fantasy life and to keep anxiety-producing thoughts away from her awareness. Hence, under stressful circumstances she was not prone to exaggerate future fears. Tasks were supposed to be tackled, not worried over. She relied on specific and selective attention, forming step-by-step conjectures and using self-instruction. This realistic approach allowed her to tolerate the high degree of frustration following her losses and deep disappointments, including the pain of her husband's death. Difficulties of daily living were not perceived as inevitably tragic or insurmountable. Distress events or setbacks seemed to be signals that mobilized coping, rather than signaling withdrawal or self-depreciation. Mood varied within a narrow range and distress seemed to cue more surveillance, control, and self-correction. She controlled emotions very carefully and chose to participate only in situations where practical action might be productive.

Coping, as expressed by perceptions, cognitions, and behavior, is a concept that interrelates with those of stress and crisis, loss and mourning, and individual support systems. Coping actions directed toward adaptation and health and expressed at different levels consist of changing a stressful situation, redefining its significance when a problem exists, and attempting to manage the stress one is experiencing. Mental health professionals will need knowledge of specific coping mechanisms in order to diagnose and help disaster victims achieve adaptation and avoid emotional impairment.

The four key concepts presented in this chapter are the essential foundation of basic knowledge that mental health workers need to understand disaster reactions and to help victims suffering from emotional consequences. As has been seen, stress and crisis, loss and mourning, systems of social and emotional supports, and coping and adaptation are overlapping notions that may be applied to disaster behavior.

An individual who has lived through a flood, hurricane, earthquake, or tornado experiences the stresses of the tragedy itself, as well as the stresses of the social consequences of the event, i.e., death, property loss, and relocation. These tensions may produce a crisis for the victim that may have either positive or negative behavioral outcomes. Coping with a personal crisis due to a disaster depends, to a great extent, upon the degree of loss sustained by the individual and the presence of one's system of social and emotional support.

In reviewing these key concepts commonly used in mental health practice, the authors suggest their applicability to disaster-related emotional reactions. Although there is a paucity of theories to explain the psychological consequences of a calamity, and since this topic is controversial in some circles, the need to develop a conceptual framework to view these behaviors is essential. This chapter presents four interrelated concepts, viewed as basic knowledge for understanding the issue; the next chapter reviews the findings of disaster research, in order to gain a better insight into the range of applied knowledge on the subject. With these knowledge presentations, basic and applied, the authors will present two models of disaster behavior in the next section. Mental health practitioners, then, can use this information to provide effective mental health services to victims of a catastrophe in their communities.

3

APPLIED CONCEPTS IN UNDERSTANDING DISASTER BEHAVIOR

When disaster strikes, the mental health professional is faced with a number of questions, such as "Where can I find information about the types of problems people experience after a catastrophe?" and "What will help me understand how a disaster survivor may behave?" This chapter addresses these and other questions through a review of disaster-related research that specifies the types of behavior observed under a variety of conditions, and through a presentation of two interrelated models designed to explain these reactions.

Not much research is available on the emotional consequences of disasters. Most extant literature reviews behavioral reactions from differing perspectives, such as psychological, intrapsychic, and sociological. For some, the idea of any serious psychological response to a catastrophe is a hotly debated issue. Mental health researchers in the past have not given enough serious attention to documenting these outcomes, so there is now a need for continued, careful investigation.

Most of the past observations and studies of disaster survivors note specific emotional outcomes by using a framework of disaster phases. These time elements consist of the preimpact, impact, and postimpact dimensions of a natural mishap. In other words, one's response depends upon the conditions of a particular phase. This factor has great importance to the mental health professional who plans to intervene therapeutically.

The authors intend to integrate the basic concepts illustrated in the previous chapter with the various research findings reviewed in this chapter by presenting two models of disaster behavior. These models incorporate the time phases of a calamity and the concepts of crisis and stress, loss and mourning, support systems, and coping, along with several additional psychological and sociological factors. By this attempted synthesis, we hope that mental health practitioners may begin to formulate some cause-and-effect theories of the emotional consequences of a calamity.

DISASTER-RELATED BEHAVIOR

The subject of the psychological consequences of a disaster has not been a popular one for mental health researchers. Most of the disaster literature available focuses on the sociological variables, emphasizing the organization of emergency relief, the impacts on the existing social structure, the roles of victims and relief workers, and better ways to plan and organize emergency programs. The little that has been written about disaster behavior has not always been systematic, nor comparable in terms of design, variables used, or general conclusions. Some authors even claim that there is little or no psychological impact from a natural disaster, leading them to believe that the topic of behavioral reactions to disaster is, at best, controversial.

However, there is some evidence in the literature to support the common belief among mental health practitioners that serious psychological implications do result from a devastating calamity. Lindemann was one of the first to explore this subject in his analysis of the behavior of individuals after the Coconut Grove fire in Boston (Lindemann, 1944). Others who have followed this viewpoint are Lifton (1967), with his study of victims of Hiroshima, a man-made disaster; Erikson (1976), with his work after the Buffalo Creek flood; and analyses by Cohen (1976), and Ahearn and Rizo Castellón (1978) of psychiatric admissions after the Managua, Nicaragua, earthquake. The question to be posed is "How do individuals react in the face of an event that could be considered cataclysmic?"

The emotional consequences of a disaster depend on many factors. These include the type and duration of the calamity, the length and type of prior warning and experience, the amount of destruction, the number of persons killed, and the way all of this is perceived and interpreted by the victim. All these factors may affect the intensity and scope of psychological impact (Fritz, 1967). As the initial, commonly observed reaction is a temporary state of shock, people may act stunned, confused, and somewhat disoriented—a state that may persist for minutes or hours (Wallace, 1957).

In a study of victims of Hurricane Audrey, people were asked to recall their thoughts during the period of impact. Many were apparently so overcome with the shock of the situation and with the struggle for immediate survival that they remembered little of what had transpired during this period (Fogleman and Parenton, 1959). A shock reaction may be regarded as normal when considered in the context of extreme loss and destruction. Psychologically, drastic events seem to have a narcotic effect, which temporarily prevents people from comprehending how much the world and their positions in it are changed (Moore, 1956).

At the time of the catastrophe, each individual is confronted with the difficulty of interpreting a new and perhaps horrifying reality. The common tendency is to associate disaster signs with normal and familiar events. The inclination to assimilate disaster clues to a normal definition is particularly common in an instantaneous disaster, or in one where the precipitating agent is unknown. At times a warning of impending danger is given, but this is typically ignored. This problem of accurate interpretation of reality is also increased when the victim has had no prior disaster experience (Kilpatrick, 1957; Fritz, 1961). An example of this is reflected in the following case study:

> It was a nightmare. The South Fork Dam had burst, and water rushed into the Conemaugh Valley and toward Johnstown. Immediately a warning of danger was transmitted by telegraph to Johnstown. As soon as she received the message, Mrs. Ogle, the manager of the Western Union Office, set out to relay the news of the impending danger just as she had done many other times in the past. Why would Johnstown ignore Mrs. Ogle's warning, an act that resulted in 2,200 deaths? According to *Harpers Weekly* of June 15, 1889: "Thousands of people discredited the alarm because it was like the false warnings they had heard before" (Gelman and Jackson, 1976).

Another example happened more recently:

> Hurricane David was an extremely dangerous force as it approached Miami in September 1979. With its winds of 140 to 150 mph, it was the most intense tropical storm to threaten the Caribbean this century. Thousands were killed in the islands of Dominica, Hispaniola (Dominican Republic and Haiti), St. Lucia, Barbados, and Martinique.
>
> When the National Hurricane Center announced a hurricane warning from Dade County, officials began the evacuation of thousands of residents. Between 5,000 and 6,000 elderly were taken from South Miami Beach to Red Cross shelters. Another 20,000 residents sought shelter at other hurricane centers to await the passage of David.
>
> The storm passed about thirty-five miles to the east of Miami, traveling on a north-to-northeast course. Some gusts to 60 mph were reported on Miami Beach and in northern Dade County, but the area had been spared the full effects of the storm.
>
> Officials were pleased that David avoided the area. They were also pleased at the efficiency of their planning and evacuation measures. Everything had gone off without any major problems. But soon after, a psychologist indicated that the near-miss was a poor psychological reinforcement for those who heeded the warning and had evacuated. He expressed the fear that in future

storms some people will disregard alarms and simply shrug them off as not serious.

Some have begun to ask what emotional effects a near-miss has. No one seems to know, but the speculation is that something happens. The most notable reaction after David was anger. One man, age 70, stated, after spending a night in an overcrowded, smelly center: "I had a better time in the trenches of World War I" (Dade County Civil Defense Division Report, 1980).

During a crisis, there is a chance that certain myths may influence an individual's perception. One of these is the *myth of personal invulnerability*, which leads one to believe that while the destructive force is real, the individual will not be hurt. When this myth cannot be sustained, it may be replaced by the *illusion of centrality*, or the feelings that the destructive forces have been aimed exclusively at the individual (McGonagle, 1964). Both myths distort reality and are harmful, to the extent that they prevent the victim from coping with reality and adopting an appropriate behavioral response. Interestingly, these myths may also continue long after the impact of the disaster and may influence one's behavior weeks or even months later.

In addition to the perceptual problems, there are also psychophysiological factors that affect individual behavior soon after a disaster. While the emotional responses of individuals vary, there seems to be general consensus that the dominant emotion expressed by victims is fear. This may be manifested by instinctual flight for family and self-preservation, a crowd psychology feeling of safety in togetherness, and high suggestibility. Some, in more serious cases, may also experience psychic numbing, hallucinations, and delusions (Fritz, 1961).

Disaster victims are almost always quiet, undemanding, and thoughtful in their dealings with other victims and disaster workers (Wallace, 1957). However, this docile manner should not be equated with a helpless, irresponsible, or dependent attitude. According to Quarantelli (1960), this "dependency image," which depicts victims as helpless and irresponsible, is a false view of their behavior.

Hostility and irritability are seldom associated with the quiet and unassuming manner of most disaster victims. These feelings, when expressed immediately after a calamity, are usually the result of widespread resentment that existed prior to the disaster (Fritz and Williams, 1957). It should be added that these feelings become more evident weeks or months later, especially if promises made by disaster workers remain unfulfilled.

Another false image of disaster behavior is the "panic image." The popular notion that catastrophe brings about panic is generally refuted in studies of disaster behavior. When flight does occur, it does not manifest itself in the way suggested by the panic image. Panic, a relatively infrequent form of behavior on the part of persons in the impact area, tends to occur only when a person or group is directly threatened by danger, or when a person defines the situation as one in which escape may be impossible. A more frequent response to danger is flight, as this is usually the only rational choice (Quarantelli and Dynes, 1970; Fritz, 1957).

In his eyewitness account of the San Francisco earthquake published May 5, 1906, in *Collier's Weekly*, Jack London described the absence of panic as follows:

> Remarkable as it may seem, Wednesday night, while the whole city crashed and roared into ruin, was a quiet night. There were no crowds. There was no shouting and yelling. There was no hysteria, no disorder. I passed Wednesday night in the path of the advancing flames, and in all those terrible hours I saw not one woman who wept, not one man who was excited, not one person who was in the slightest degree panic-stricken.

In general, human behavior seems to be adaptive. People take actions to protect themselves and others, rather than engage in irrational acts that are likely to increase danger. Much of the initial rescue work is often done by disaster victims themselves; Mutual and self-help are frequent. Even on the part of persons who are in the epicenter of a calamity, goal-oriented forms of behavior are much more common than the uncontrolled, irrational types (Fritz, 1957; McGonagle, 1964).

While the general tendency may be toward adaptive behavior, little information is available to explain the types of psychological problems that some victims experience. General statistics describing human response to disaster indicate that 15 to 25 percent of the involved population are able to evaluate their situation and take prompt, effective action that is sustained and continued in adaptive behavior. The remaining percentage of victims react in a stunned and bewildered fashion for varying periods of time. An hour or so after impact, the majority will usually respond appropriately, while approximately 15 percent of the total may take a day or two to adopt purposeful behavior. It is in this latter group where disorientation, confusion, crying, paralyzing anxiety, and hysteria occur. These reactions may persist for an undeterminable length of time (Fritz and Williams, 1957). Following is an example of such a victim:

> Mrs. S., a 45-year-old widow rescued from a rooftop after a severe flooding. She had remained alone in the darkness for four hours waiting for the rescue boat to approach her house and find her. She was holding a small dog, which she handed to the fireman who helped her into the boat. The dog fell in the rushing waters and disappeared. Mrs. S. struggled to "command" the boat to turn back and when this was denied, started crying inconsolably for the rest of the trip to the shelter. There she accepted all orders and suggestions in a very docile manner but paced up and down the shelter continuously. She refused to eat for two days and would only talk about the rescue event.

After allowing her to ventilate and share her feelings, she began to plan for the next action steps necessary for relocation.

Most studies of disaster-related behavior are organized in terms of time sequence. While there are variations, the general format usually relates to preimpact, impact, and postimpact phases. The first phase, preimpact, includes a number of important factors, such as the type of warning given and the response to it, a person's prior disaster experience, and the degree of individual stress present prior to the catastrophe. The second phase, impact, involves the immediate behavioral responses to different types of disasters, while the third, or postimpact, phase refers to the degree of community disorganization and how victims continue to adjust. For mental health practitioners an understanding of each phase and its influence on human behavior is important for both planning and intervention.

A variety of emotional responses has been noted earlier for the impact phase. These reactions, according to many, continue for weeks and months later into the postimpact period. Authors usually discuss the final disaster phase as the time when the victim comes face-to-face with daily life in an environment that has been radically changed. An experience of extreme danger and personal vulnerability is not over once the calamity is past, even for those who have adapted well and survived. It is something that requires time to assimilate. In the aftermath of a disaster, people may be afflicted with a tormenting memory of the event and an intense fear of its recurrence (Wolfstein, 1957).

For many, the first overt emotional expression occurs during the beginning of the postimpact phase, sometimes called the period of recoil. At this time, there is a need to be with others and to ventilate feelings related to the shocking sense of loss or perhaps loneliness (Tyhurst, 1951). Usually victims have a great desire to talk and to relate their disaster experiences. When immediate emotional expression is delayed, the victims may demonstrate underactivity, helpless and aimless wandering, dazed apathy, or depressed behavior. A more extreme reaction may be the "shocked" response evident when an individual is unable to communicate normally (Healy, 1969). At this point, both the character of individual responses and their management by relief workers would appear to have crucial significance for subsequent psychological events. Many believe that professional mental health attention at this time would not only assist victims in distress but also facilitate a speedy recovery from a temporary breakdown (Tyhurst, 1951).

The period of recoil described above is followed by what some refer to as the posttraumatic phase. Hypothetically, this is part of the postimpact period and may continue for the remainder of a person's life. Reactions associated with this period include temporary, fluctuating anxiety, fatigue states, psychotic episodes, recurrent catastrophic dreaming, and depressive reactions. The more severe and prolonged expressions of these symptoms have been referred to as "traumatic syndrome" or "posttraumatic neuroses" (Tyhurst, 1951).

Another researcher, in describing this phase, has noted that victims may experience insomnia, digestive upsets, nervousness, and other physical complaints. More serious behavioral expressions may be a depressed reaction manifested by apparent lack of emotion, vacant expression, or motionless behavior. Overactive responses may be an argumentative manner, rapid talking, loss of judgment, uncontrollable weeping, or wild running about. There may also be bodily reactions such as severe nausea, vomiting, and conversion hysteria (Healy, 1969).

The postimpact or posttraumatic period has been interpreted as a phase in which a number of long-range emotional problems occur. Lifton, in his book, *Death in Life,* studies the long-term psychological problems of victims of a man-made disaster, namely the bombing of Hiroshima (Lifton, 1967). In his analysis, Lifton develops five themes to understand better the behavior of survivors. These general themes are: death imprint, death guilt, psychic numbing, nurturance and contagion, and formulation.

The basis of all survivor themes is the imprint of death. With a jarring awareness of death, the victims may respond either with a heightened vulnerability or with a sense of reinforced invulnerability resulting from having met death and conquered it. Related to death imprint is a "death spell," which may present itself in a fascination with scenes of death and later with an indelible image of the death encounter. The early symptoms of this have been described as characteristics of acute grief, which includes preoccupation with death, guilt, bodily complaints, and hostile behavior.

Survival experience is usually accompanied by a severe sense of guilt. This may result from the feeling that one's survival was purchased at the expense of another. The victim's major defense against death guilt is a cessation of feeling, or psychic numbing. This is a process of protecting oneself from a sense of complete helplessness and from a feeling that an unmanageable force has invaded the person. However, while psychic numbing begins as a defense mechanism, when it fails it may overwhelm the individual with death imagery. Becoming entrapped by a continuous threat or preoccupation with death, the disaster victim may only be able to express or dispel his feelings through nonverbal means or by demonstrating additional psychiatric symptomology.

The survivor's general outlook and his personal relationships may be influenced by a suspicion of counterfeit nurturance and a perception of others' fear of contagion. Suspicion can cause the victim to feel abused by everyone, particularly by those most involved in giving help. Contagion anxiety may foster a sense of exclusiveness among survivors based upon shared experiences and the "knowledge of death."

Ultimately, the individual survivor must engage in a process of formulation by reestablishing from within a definition of oneself with respect to the "new reality." This formulative effort is the victim's attempt to return from the trauma of a disaster and to begin establishing coping patterns necessary to begin life anew.*

Several studies of disasters contribute to our understanding of the postimpact stage. One is Erikson's fine analysis of the emotional consequences of the Buffalo Creek flood. Noting that a range of psychiatric problems was found after the catastrophe, the author concluded that although some were the direct result of the disaster itself, many problems resulted from the social disorganization caused by the calamity. The process of relocation, living in an unfamiliar environment, and beginning life again without a loved one or without a job were viewed as additional stresses that produced psychological problems. The impact of social disorganization in the aftermath of a catastrophe has been referred to as "the second disaster" (Erikson, 1976).

More specific data on emotional responses are presented in a study of psychiatric admissions after the earthquake of Managua, Nicaragua (Ahearn and Rizo Castellón, 1978). By comparing pre- and postdisaster admission rates in the only psychiatric hospital in the country, the researchers found that admissions increased by 27 percent after the catastrophe. The study confirmed earlier investigations that neurotic symptoms are common following a calamity. In Managua, postdisaster admissions for neurosis rose by 46 percent for the year, although the increase was 209 percent in the first three months afterward. Interestingly, the forms of neurosis with the largest increases included anxiety, depressive reactions, and hysteria. The typical patient with these problems were young mothers.

Other findings of the Managua study are instructive. For instance, new cases of psychosis declined 17 percent, while readmissions jumped 49 percent in the postearthquake year. For some reason, a natural disaster does not produce psychosis, but it is obvious that individuals with a previous history of serious psychiatric impairment will be markedly vulnerable to the trauma of disaster and its after-effects. Another finding fits well with Erikson's "second disaster" theory. Postearthquake admissions for cerebral organic syndromes increased by 42.4 percent, while those for mental retardation rose by 35.4 percent. As a disaster does not produce cerebral organic syndrome or, for that matter, mental retardation, could it be that these admissions increased because of the social disorganization after the earthquake? Under conditions of relocation, did families encounter special problems in caring for one of their members because they had to live with relatives, in a tent, or in a

*Evelyn J. Bromet and Charles Schulberg, two researchers from the University of Pittsburgh, have begun a study of Three Mile Island, near Harrisburg, Pa. Their concern is the psychological behavior and social aspects of the nuclear accident.

refugee camp? In addition, is it also possible that as other service resources—such as hospitals, pharmacies, and the services of local physicians—were destroyed, families sought help from the one source that was available and accessible—the psychiatric hospital? It certainly appears so.

Finally, there was a drop of 34 percent in admissions for personality disorders the year after the Managuan catastrophe. The decline of deviant behavior was explained by two possible factors: first, that the actual incidence of deviance declined, and, secondly, that societal norms were relaxed in the disaster's aftermath to the extent that former definitions of deviance were no longer operative.

Although the literature on the subject is sparse, and research studies differ in focus and methodology, there does seem to be mounting evidence that disasters produce or influence emotional problems. This section has reviewed the range of behavioral consequences that may result from disasters. Mental health practitioners should be familiar with the range of behavioral responses that are possible in the face of catastrophe. They should also realize that emotional problems change over time and are associated with a host of human phenomena, such as crisis, stress, coping, and support systems, as presented and discussed in the last section.

MODELS OF DISASTER-RELATED BEHAVIOR

Mental health professionals have usually maintained that natural disasters produce or influence psychological reactions in their victims. We agree with this proposition. Although the exact cause-and-effect relationships are not well defined, concepts of crisis and stress, loss and mourning, social and emotional resources, and coping and adaptation are frequently used to explain the emotional implications of natural calamities.

The authors will present two models based upon the concepts described in Chapter 2 and applied experience as described in the first part of this chapter. These models explain the phenomenology of disaster-related behavior as a guide to intervention. Although the models overlap, they do present the reader with two distinct perspectives.

Influences of Disaster-Related Behavior

Figure 1 is a diagram of each of these conceptual elements that attempts to explain the behavioral outcomes of a disaster. It is assumed that a natural catastrophe such as an earthquake is a crisis event that impacts personal equilibrium and produces severe stress. At the moment of the calamity, a victim's behavior will depend on a number of prior

FIGURE 1. Paradigm of influences on disaster-related behavior

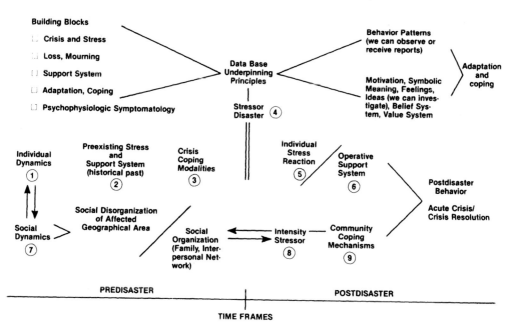

factors, as well as the victim's interpretation and definition of the threatening event. Prior to the disaster, certain individuals may have been exposed to other crises or events, such as divorce, the birth of a child, or relocation, indicating that they may be particularly vulnerable to another crisis. Another factor is whether or not the individual has had previous successful coping experience and previous disaster experience. Those with the former may have additional skills that would enable them to cope better with a disaster crisis, and those with the latter experience might be able to interpret disaster signs better and more effectively manage the stress associated with calamities. In effect, prior experience, as well as the predisaster emotional and physical state, will influence the way victims cope with a natural disaster and its consequences.

The initial impact of a disaster is a crisis event that may produce extraordinary stress (S_1 in figure 1). Whether a victim presents psychological impairment depends on several factors:

- Type and duration of the disaster;
- Degree of loss;
- The victim's role, coping skill, and support system; and
- The survivor's perception and interpretation of the catastrophe.

Some natural calamities, such as earthquakes, are sudden and short lived, while others, such as floods and hurricanes, develop slowly and have a relatively long duration. This latter group of natural hazards usually involves warnings that are typically ignored or denied. Individuals judge the degree of jeopardy as they define the nature of the disaster and its potential threat to self and family. Their behavioral response at the moment of impact and in the first hours or days afterward will also be associated with:

- Their degree of loss (death of loved one, loss of home or job);
- Their role and the behavior expected of them by others;
- The presence or absence of emotional resources and a supportive social network or relationships; and
- Their skill and ability to cope with the stress of the natural disaster.

Some time later the victim will confront the new social reality of having to adjust and begin life anew. This period, referred to earlier as the "second disaster," produces stress and adds to that of the impact phase. In figure 1 this stress is noted as S_2. The source of this stress is the crisis that emanates from a destroyed environment and the resulting social disorganization. Victims no longer have the familiarity of their neighborhoods and may have to face the rigor of relocation. They may also continue to mourn the loss of a loved one, or they may have lost their supportive networks, or their jobs. Each of these factors causes sudden role changes, produces hardships in readjustment, and radically alters social interrelationships. The stress, or S_2, that results from the aftermath of disaster may also be a cause of psychophysiological symptoms.

It is also conceivable that some individuals who are not initial victims of the disaster may be exposed to conditions of the postdisaster phase and may experience crisis and severe stress, noted as S_3. In large disasters, people in neighboring towns may feel the effects of relocation of victims as they house relatives, or as their towns take in hundreds or thousands of refugees. Also, if the region's economy is impacted by the calamity, nondisaster victims may suffer from job loss or reduction in income. Still others may have lost loved ones and reacted with a protracted grieving process. As described in figure 1, these individuals may also experience crisis effects as disaster exposes them to severe stress.

Conceptual Model for Disaster-Related Intervention

Conceptual model 2 involves the organization and building of a theoretical knowledge base in order to understand the interrelationships between the dynamic forces, coping resources, and crisis that characterize an individual after a disaster. The model involves using this understanding to develop procedures and methods of crisis counseling.

This model explains, through the use of several interrelated concepts, individual crisis after a disaster and appropriate areas of psychological intervention. We hope that the model will highlight the dynamic interplay of the catastrophe and its effects, the victim's characteristics, and the environment in which the hazardous event takes place. We will use the following principles:

- Bereavement and loss reactions follow disasters when they affect an individual by producing a loss of person, property, or environment;
- Individuals vary in levels of adaptation to new situations and environments;
- Crisis symptoms are produced by and in turn affect social, psychological, and physiological disorganization, and all of this can be studied as an interrelated process;
- Postdisaster victims need social, psychological, physiological, and economic help; and
- The after-effects of crisis resolution can be long term, and are moderate, minimal, or severe, depending on the adaptive/nonadaptive resolution of demands placed on an individual as a result of the disaster.

These principles should be considered when linking the concepts presented in figure 2. There is a basic body of knowledge from which concepts can be correlated to take into account the systemic relationships and interdependent effects involved in the behavior of individuals after a disaster. Calamity victims will manifest behaviors that indicate the level of adaptation available to them through personal actions, feelings (sense of hope vs. hopelessness), and energy levels. The outcome can be better understood if one investigates the antecedent variables that characterize an individual's social, psychological, and physiological constitution. People face a disaster with a set of coping mechanisms and previous historical events that have left them with an array of psychophysiological adaptive mechanisms. The level of functional disorganization in which they find themselves after the event, and the subsequent recovery and restitution activities that will influence their lives, are related causally to the disaster. The concept of support systems balanced against the crisis outcome is clearly manifested in this situation. The psychological intervention that can be offered must be directed at two levels—the individual and the community. The major objective of mental health professional activities is to strengthen adaptation mechanisms on an individual level and to assist in developing support disaster-recovery systems in the community in such a way that they fit individuals' needs and make their progress easier.

Figure 2 presents theoretical arrangements of basic knowledge concepts and organizes data to guide the professional in developing procedures to meet this objective.

The individual whose life patterns have suddenly been disrupted due to a calamity and who is offered new living arrangements has to develop a coping behavior to adapt to the emergency and the changing situation.

FIGURE 2. Conceptual model for disaster intervention

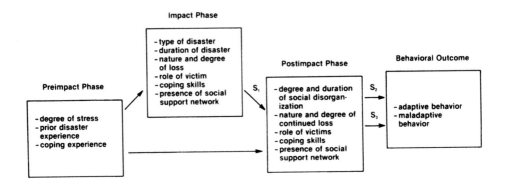

Stress₁ - produced solely by the disaster itself
Stress₂ - caused by the disaster as well as the subsequent community disorganization
Stress₃ - the result of community disorganization

Psychological observation and interviewing techniques can be used to understand this set of behaviors, in order to evaluate the degree of distress so that assistance and support might be offered. In this way data can be collected to identify the following conditions, which are numbered to correspond with our conceptual model for disaster behavior. These conditions are:

1. Individual personality characteristics;
2. Type of historical events through which the victim has achieved his or her level of development;
3. Individual's usual coping mechanisms and available methods to deal with crisis;
4. History of the disaster and how it has affected the individual from his perspective;
5. Reactive behavior and personality skills to adapt to the new post-disaster situation;
6. Social and community system of supports available to victims and the use they make of these resources;
7. The level of support available through community and disaster assistance agencies, given the degree of social disorganization;
8. The intensity of stressors, related to the balance between the severity of the disaster and the availability of support resources;

9. The nature of this balance, which will support and enhance or undermine the quality of coping resources.

Information from each step clarifies the victim's behavior as well as his vulnerability to disaster stress and his specific requirements to regain equilibrium. In addition, it helps us understand the social/economic environment from which the victim came and in which he now finds himself. This set of variables is important in the planning of a crisis resolution strategy.

Theoretically, the individual calls on his own personality skills to adapt. If he is unable to deal with the multiple events brought on by the catastrophe, he next tries to extend his sources of support, accepting recovery agency assistance. If these resources are unavailable or inadequate to meet life-event demands produced by the disaster, the individual may then turn to his culturally provided beliefs, values, and symbols. In postdisaster behavior we see individuals who take advantage of all available resources simultaneously and in a complementary manner.

At each of these points, the mental health professional has an opportunity to offer assistance to the individual within his social matrix. The professional will find, at some point of crisis resolution, a juncture that leads toward a healthy or pathological end point. The mental health professional must possess the skills and the knowledge to assess the situation and to bring to bear therapeutic interventive procedures which support and guide the victim toward achieving the best potential outcome within the situation engendered by disaster in a specific community.

In summary, mental health workers may expect emotional problems from the impact of a hazard as victims experience fear, shock, psychic numbing, anxiety, depression, and psychosomatic complaints. In the aftermath of a disaster and as weeks and months go by, some victims are not able to cope with their problems and continue to express anxiety, depression, anger, nightmares, insomnia, and difficulty in interpersonal relations. Also, in the aftermath persons other than victims may be exposed to disaster stress and express emotional problems. Relatives of victims, residents of neighboring towns, and disaster relief workers are groups vulnerable to the consequences of disaster stress. Finally, the models presented in figures 1 and 2 are ways to assemble disaster-related behavior for the purposes of psychological intervention, if required.

4

HOW TO PLAN AND IMPLEMENT A
MENTAL HEALTH SERVICE
AFTER A DISASTER

This chapter describes a model for the development and implementation of mental health services to help victims suffering from the psychological consequences of a disaster. Mental health administrators facing the chaos of the catastrophe's aftermath and needing knowledge to act as soon as possible frequently find themselves perplexed and unsure as to what actions are necessary. Although responses may differ from disaster to disaster, it is possible to develop a guide for the design and execution of psychological assistance to survivors of calamities. Administrators can use this guide, applied flexibly, as a means to review the necessary activities for promptly and effectively delivering service to those in need.

Through a thorough and clear understanding of the emotional implications of a disaster, mental health leaders must assume the responsibility for making the call to action, mobilizing the required resources, and planning help for victims. They must recognize how people are affected, what elements enter into the design of a plan, what coordination with other services is necessary, and how psychological aid can be effectively delivered to victims. Without this knowledge, administrators may waste valuable time deciding what the task is and how to accomplish it.

In order to help mental health managers develop and carry out a program following a disaster, this chapter reviews a model that sets forth elements in the planning and administration of a project. Specifically, this guide considers the requirements for:

- Sanction and support;
- Assessment of need;
- Setting the goals of intervention;
- Considering alternatives;
- Designing a program; and
- Implementing and running a project for mental health services.

This chapter also offers case studies that detail step-by-step elements in plan design and program maintenance. By presenting practical illustrations, the authors hope to suggest some helpful hints and recommendations for accomplishing the tasks outlined above.

GUIDE TO PLANNING A MENTAL HEALTH SERVICE

Planning in a postdisaster environment requires knowledge, patience, and flexibility. Accurate data about what has happened and who is suffering are essential, but most often the information available is sorely inadequate or difficult to gather. After a disaster, mental health leaders must work long hours deciding what to do and how to do it. In most cases they will encounter situations that are unique to their community, situations that require flexibility and innovation in their approach toward helping the victims. The following guide has been devised to assist these administrators in their efforts. Although planners may—in fact, must —work on several elements at the same time, the steps in the process are interrelated and may overlap.

Sanction and Support

Before proceeding very far, mental health administrators will need legitimation and sanction for their actions. In some instances these administrators may possess authority by virtue of position or legal status, but in other instances they may have to seek approval actively in order to start a mental health service for disaster victims. At the regional level, the person who usually has the authority to sanction action is the Community Mental Health Center (CMHC) director, or the director of a catchment area. If additional authority is required, administrators may seek the approval and assistance of the director or commissioner of the state's mental health department. Lack of early legitimation creates a situation in which conflict and competition may ensue, thus lowering the chances of success. The following example is illustrative:

> The idea of a mental health intervention project after the earthquake in Managua, Nicaragua, came independently from two professionals, a psychologist and a psychiatrist. Unaware of each other, both called the International Desk of the National Institutes of Mental Health (NIMH) to explore the possibilities of a project and to gain the support of this agency. Agreeing that such a project was interesting and worthwhile, a representative of NIMH traveled to Nicaragua with one of the callers to seek approval and sanction for a joint program to assist the disaster victims. They met with government officials, representatives of the local psychiatric association, and mental health workers to discuss the project. All gave enthusiastic approval. When the U.S. mental health team arrived in April 1973, its members continued the process of solidifying sanction for the project through further discussions with the

groups mentioned above. (In addition, they met with the wife of the country's president and she became the project's sponsor.)

When this team left Managua at the end of April 1973, one of its members spoke to the local Nicaraguan press, saying that the political regime was not only repressive but was also guilty of profiting from the aid sent by other nations to the earthquake refugees. When the team arrived in the United States, these comments were repeated to the *New York Times*. Because of the adverse publicity both in Nicaragua and the United States, official action toward the mental health team was predictable and swift. The project lost formal sanction to continue.

A second U.S. team arrived in May 1973 and had to deal with the loss of formal sanction. Its members considered terminating both the project and any efforts to regain full sanction so as to continue. Obviously the formal sanction was diminished, but could enough informal support be secured to reactivate the project? They were not sure. However, by returning to discuss the matter with mental health professionals (who valued the need for these services), psychiatric leaders, and interested agency officials, their month-long efforts paid off. They got enough informal support to continue the project—even without the formal sanction of the Nicaraguan government.

The second U.S. team left Managua in August 1973 after working with their Nicaraguan counterparts to set up ten community mental health centers for the earthquake's 300,000 refugees. When the project ended six months later, more than 7,000 victims had received some form of psychiatric assistance from these clinics through the efforts of thirty-one Nicaraguan mental health professionals and their North American counterparts.

The mental health leader may take several immediate actions toward securing sanction. First, regional or state mental health officials should be contacted by telephone to communicate an assessment of the disaster's consequences and the need for action. These calls should be followed up with meetings, if possible, to clarify issues of sanction and responsibility. For instance, the lines of authority and the delineation of responsibilities must be clear to all. State and regional officials will often ask for an on-site tour of the disaster area for purposes of surveying what has happened and deciding if a program should be initiated. Finally, approval to act should be put in writing to avoid confusion or conflict later.

Associated with this need for legitimation is the need for formal and informal support at all levels of one's efforts. Mental health activities following a calamity obviously cannot operate in a vacuum but must be interrelated with a variety of relief services. Because mental health service has only recently emerged as a participant in the system of relief, the support of other care-giving groups and organizations is essential. To enter the relief system with mental health services requires the approval and support of authorities—for example, managers of shelters and hotels and Federal Emergency Management Administration officials. Additionally, in an effort to mobilize both manpower and financial resources, mental health administrators will want to seek the support of health and human services organizations and their community workers. Agreements with agencies and with individual professionals may be formal or informal, but both must serve the purpose of securing cooperation toward aiding disaster victims and organizing the necessary personnel, equipment, and funds for action. These arrangements are usually made by telephone or at informal or formal meetings. They are seldom arranged in writing due to time limitations. An illustration of this follows:

In February 1978, Massachusetts suffered from a now historic blizzard that produced devastating tidal floods along the state's coastline. Because of the extent of property destruction and the large number of people made homeless by the storm, President Carter declared Massachusetts a disaster area. Various mental health practitioners responded quickly to the emergency in hopes of providing psychological aid to those in need. However, they soon encountered the need to legitimate their role to other disaster workers.

One of the mental health professionals who volunteered was a psychiatrist and director of a mental health catchment area which included a community that had sustained serious harm from the disaster. As she entered the principal refugee shelter in this area, she observed representatives from the Red Cross and from various levels of government milling around trying to develop cohesive planning procedures and to clarify their roles. The scene was one of confusion. She invited a small group of these relief workers to gather in an adjoining room and took several minutes to explain who she was and what resources she could bring to the situation. Producing a copy of the federal regulations on disasters which indicate that crisis intervention and counseling are part of the relief effort, she was able to orient other workers to her role and her possible contribution, thus gaining their support and acceptance as a team member.

This psychiatrist continued her work at the shelter for several weeks, receiving the positive and open collaboration of the other relief workers. Without their legitimation and referral assistance, the psychiatrist would have been an isolated member of the relief team.

One way to maintain support and legitimacy for a mental health project throughout the disaster effort is to establish, as soon as possible, a task force to help plan and operate the project. In organizing such a committee, one should try to recruit individuals from various levels of the mental health services, the human services, and the community at large. A task force may vary from twelve to twenty-five members, with fifteen to eighteen suggested. These individuals should represent four distinct elements of the community:

- Experts: Professionals in mental health and human services who have knowledge of the emotional consequences of disaster and of ways to provide psychological aid;

- Power group: Individuals who, by virtue of their position or social status, have influence in the community and are able to facilitate decisions to grant resources or support (examples include politicians, businessmen, or clergy);
- Sentiment group: Members of the larger community, such as civic and socal groups that do not usually initiate action but have the power to block something with which they disagree. These groups reflect the broad values, norms, and sentiment of the community and include the League of Women Voters, Rotary Club, or local unions;
- Needs group: Individuals who know the problem first hand, i.e., disaster victims (Burke, 1979).

Such a task force can help a proposed mental health project secure legitimation and financial support, interpret need, shape program goals, and publicize its services to the community at large.

Assessment of Need

Any plan to give psychological aid should be responsive to the specific problems of disaster victims. To do this, mental health planners should:
- Understand the community's definition of health and illness;
- Survey existing problems to determine the nature and extent of those problems, as well as the groups affected;
- Ascertain the community resources available to combat the problems; and
- Use these data to help set program goals and strategies.

The way one defines a social problem is important in assessing need. Because these definitions often depend upon the interaction of norms and values, and on culture and tradition, different communities delineate problems differently. In the area of mental health, the view of what constitutes health and illness is important. Acceptable behavior in one community may be classified as deviant in another. Therefore mental health planners, especially those from outside the impacted community, must be sensitive to these distinctions when assessing need.

Methods to gain information about the problems of victims vary, but they usually combine a study of reactions from other calamities and a sampling of actual problems in one's community. At a very early stage, mental health practitioners should review the literature on disaster behavior to familiarize themselves with the typical symptoms that victims may present. Reports of other mental health projects designed after a catastrophe, detailing the types of reactions experienced by victims, are also helpful. Usually such reports may be obtained through the disaster unit of NIMH* or directly from the community mental health center in the impacted area.

Mental health professionals will also need to survey in the field the kinds of emotional impairment suffered in the community by victims. Strategies to collect this information can be both formal and informal. By setting up temporary mental health stations in shelters, refugee camps, and affected areas, practitioners can gain in a short time an understanding of victims' problems. They should remember, however, that the nature and degree of these problems change over time. Another useful technique is a careful review of case records at mental health clinics and facilities to discover the types of symptoms expressed by individuals. A more informal approach is to talk with mental health and disaster workers in order to review and analyze their observations of postcatastrophe behavior.

As an example, a rapid, practical approach to the assessment of need was used in the aftermath of the Managuan earthquake. U.S. volunteers and Nicaraguan mental health professionals formed teams that were deployed at key points in the devastated areas, such as refugee camps, hospitals, clinics, and centers operated by volunteers and religious groups. Each team gathered data from the patients seen and sent those statistics to the project headquarters. Here the data were aggregated according to frequency, sex, age, type of problem, and service needed. Within a week, this system of documentation gave ample evidence of the increasing need of Managuans for mental health assistance. It also permitted a crude estimate of the total number of postdisaster emotional casualties.

In assessing need, administrators and planners will have to know some specific facts about victims and their problems. A formal or informal guide constructed to survey need should include the following information, which will become essential in making program decisions later. These data are:

- Background information, i.e., age, marital status, education, number of children, address, etc.;
- Presenting symptoms (classified in broad general categories to avoid psychiatric labeling);
- Degree of loss from calamity, i.e., death of family or friends, destruction of home or property, or loss of income or employment;
- Mental health status prior to disaster, i.e., degree of stress, coping skill, prior mental health treatment; and
- The victim's system of social and psychological supports.

*The full name of the unit is the Disaster Assistance and Emergency Mental Health Section, Division of Special Mental Health Programs, National Institutes of Mental Health, 5600 Fishers Lane, Rockville, Maryland, 20852.

In seeking victims in the field, the practitioner seldom has the time to do a complete history and make a diagnosis. Generally there is only a short time, often minutes, to make a quick assessment and to note some salient facts. The list above may guide the practitioner toward using time efficiently in gaining useful and relevant data.

The major purpose of an assessment of need is to understand the problems of victims so that relevant services can be planned and provided for them. Once the behavioral outcomes of disaster have been identified, planners should try to extrapolate their data to the general population and thus determine the magnitude of problems. This is a difficult task, and many planners who lack sufficient information estimate the affected population by calculating 15 percent of the total, a percentage often cited in the literature on disasters.

A second component of the assessment process is a detailed survey of available resources in the community. Mental health planners and practitioners need to know what sources of assistance for disaster victims are available and must be able to mobilize these resources in their treatment efforts. Resources consist of available health and human services, such as local public health clinics, Family Service Associations, and the welfare department. Also included are services to help victims in securing food, shelter, financial assistance, or home repairs. Table 1 is an example of the types of services and agencies that provide help after a disaster.

The Disaster Response and Recovery Division of FEMA coordinates all relief activities after a disaster. The agency has a telephone line that provides information to victims on all available services and also operates one-stop centers that house the varied services (federal, state, and local) available to victims. Some services may also be available in shelters, hotels, trailer camps, or other places where refugees are found.

In summary, an inventory of local, state, and federal resources, when compared with existing need, highlights gaps in services. By identifying resources for disaster victims and helping mental health workers understand the system of available disaster resources, these listings are also important for planning and funding new services. Later this knowledge of system resources gains importance when the question of linking services for coordinated efforts is raised.

Goals of a Mental Health Service

In setting specific service goals, mental health experts must review and analyze the results of the assessment of need and the inventory of resources in order to complete their identification of problem areas and their listing of service priorities. Service goals should be generated from the assessment of problems and should specify priorities and groups targeted for assistance.

In most cases, a planning task force or group of mental health administrators and practitioners set program goals that emphasize service priorities. They may also consider the project's scope and duration, but these often depend upon other factors, such as funding or personnel.

TABLE 1. Organizational Resources for Services to Disaster Victims

Organizational Auspice:	Services Offered					
	Food	Shelter	Income	Health	Information	Other
Voluntary						
Red Cross	X	X	X	X	X	X
Salvation Army	X	X				X
Catholic Charities	X	X	X			X
Mennonites		X				
Local churches	X	X	X			
Local unions	X		X			X
Civic/social clubs	X		X			X
Local						
Civil defense					X	
Community action	X	X	X		X	
Health department				X		
Local hospital				X		
Mental health				X		
Mayor's office					X	
State						
Health department				X		
Mental health agency				X		
Governor's office					X	
National Guard					X	X
Community develop- ment agency		X				
Employment and security agency			X			
Federal						
Health, Education, and Welfare	X		X			
Labor			X			
Agriculture	X					
Housing and Urban Development		X			X	
Small Business Administration			X		X	

Once broad goals have been set, the planner designs specific objectives to meet each goal. By defining these operationally, program monitoring and evaluation become easier.

Alternative Program Approaches

Goals are broad statements of value and priority that may be translated into action through a variety of program strategies. Although most mental health projects will employ a number of approaches, there is usually the choice of one or two methods of intervention over the others. At this point, planners must determine the best way to achieve their goals, considering the range of options available to them. For example:

> Within a week of the Massachusetts blizzard, mental health leaders had decided to mount a program of psychological assistance, but they were unsure as to how to implement their service. Due to property destruction, refugees were scattered throughout the area. Some went to shelters, others to hotels, and still others to live with relatives. Given their goal to provide mental health services, administrators seriously considered a decentralized approach versus a centralized program. On the one hand, there was a need to identify survivors, define the levels of psychological assistance required, and spell out the alternative procedures to do this. On the other hand, there was the question of cost, time, logistics, and types of personnel needed.
>
> Which approach would be best? Each strategy had its advantages and disadvantages. Deciding to meet, the administrators reviewed all the data available, calculated the required resources and cost of each option, and, in the end, decided to decentralize their service component to the affected neighborhoods, while at the same time maintaining a centralized administrative and fiscal component.

Program alternatives can depend upon the preferred methods of treatment or different administrative structures and are chosen for the purpose of achieving the project's goals and objectives. Discussion of alternative ways to carry out the program should lead to early decision and agreement on a specific strategy. For instance, a group may believe that a short-term project, located in refugee camps and emphasizing crisis counseling, is better than a long-range program using a group therapy strategy. Perhaps a new project independent of the existing mental health system may be an alternative considered.

Program Design

Once the program's goals and objectives are clear, the priorities set, and the preference of alternatives known, the mental health administrator or planner is ready to develop the details of the project. In order to design any program, an understanding of the elements in the planning process is necessary. Four key factors—functional, technological, efficiency, and systemic requirements—should be considered (Perrow, 1967). By focusing on these factors and considering the implications of each, the administrator/planner can devise the steps necessary to design a project of psychological aid to disaster victims. In understanding these factors, the following definitions are offered.

Functional requisites consist of the identification and listing of program activities and/or services, including the specific approaches for intervention and providing assistance. Activities such as outreach, problem identification and diagnosis, and treatment modalities should be detailed.

In carrying out program functions, *technological requirements* reflect the need for financial, material, and personnel resources—for instance, type and number of staff; need for space and facilities; and equipment, materials, and furniture requirements.

A third consideration in program development is the imperative of *efficiency*. This includes formulating a design for the type of administration, accounting, information, and evaluation systems to be employed, as well as a strategy for integrating the units of service and for offering supervision. The following issues must also be decided:

- Program auspices, sponsorship, and administration;
- Centralization vs. decentralization of service;
- Program budget and costs;
- Length of project;
- Forms of accountability; and
- The nature of program supervision.

By tying the proposed effort to existing services in the community through agreements, board representation, and contracts, the mental health planner addresses the last factor in program design, *systemic requisites*. The object is to maximize project coordination with other agencies. The main ingredient of these systemic requisites is cooperative arrangements with additional programs and services in order to survive, avoid competition, and offer clients the quality of services they need. In making referral agreements, in educating the public, and in seeking financial, material, and moral support, mental health planners must link the project to existing resources in the community. As an example:

> Soon after the storm, the mental health team in Revere, Massachusetts, actively sought affiliations and agreements with other agencies. The first level of agreement was developed at the refugee shelter with the various private and governmental organizations, in order to secure collaborative referral linkages and provide case consultation. Later, as the victim population dispersed to temporary housing or the homes of relatives, the team contacted the local interagency relief council and the local mental health clinic. Through a series of personal interviews with these organizations, an agreement was reached that specified procedures for sharing information, making referrals, and exchanging resources and technical assistance.

In developing a plan to help disaster victims, it is important to remember that each step in the planning process is interrelated with all other steps. Plan design, as influenced by the assessment of need and by stated project goals and priorities, will influence the implementation stage of the plan. Each step leads to and interacts with the prior and the next step in the process. Once developed, the plan is usually approved by a committee, task force, or mental health administrator.

IMPLEMENTATION AND ADMINISTRATION OF A PROJECT

During the implementation phase, a number of issues present themselves. These include funding for the project; the selection, orientation, and training of staff; and the design of administrative and information structures. The mental health planner or project director, with the assistance of the task force, deals with each of these issues as the project progresses.

Funding

The cost of a mental health project for disaster victims will reflect the type and size of the program planned, but its financing will depend upon the ability to demonstrate need, the soundness of the proposed project, and the capacity to mobilize community resources. Although monies are available from a variety of sources to finance a mental health project for disaster victims, actual funding is usually less than expected and may be difficult to secure.

There are various funding sources, depending on one's location. In responding quickly to a disaster, there is seldom time to write a grant to secure financial backing. In most cases, the immediate program response is done with volunteers and, in time, aid is requested from the CMHC or other local sources. This aid is usually in the form of borrowed staff, equipment, and space. Later, mental health administrators may petition local or state organizations for financial help. Such sources may include the State Department of Mental Health, Catholic Charities, the Family Service Association, the local Mental Health Association, local foundations, or groups that have raised money for a relief fund.

In the case of a presidentially declared disaster, mental health leaders have another source of funding, the Disaster Assistance and Emergency Mental Health Section of NIMH. Under Section 413 of the Disaster Relief Act of 1974 (Public Law 93-288), monies are available for crisis counseling and aid to victims. Briefly, the law reads as follows:

Sec. 413. The President is authorized (through the National Institute of Mental Health) to provide professional counseling services, including financial assistance to states or local agencies or private mental health organizations to provide such services or training of disaster workers, to victims of major disasters in order to alleviate mental health problems caused or aggravated by major disasters or their aftermath.

Funds for this program actually come from FEMA, but are administered by NIMH's disaster unit. Interested administrators should contact this agency for details on applying for a grant. Current regulations permit projects for a duration of six months, but in special instances FEMA and NIMH may provide an extension of one to three months. Finally, in applying for a 413 project, a careful needs assessment that documents a need over and above the baseline of average clinic case-loads is required.

Administrative Structures

In most cases, the mental health program plan stipulates the type of administrative structures deemed necessary to deliver services to disaster victims. If this has not been done, it becomes necessary to address the issues of program auspice and sponsorship, of the types and degrees of authority, and whether the program will be centralized or decentralized. Once these decisions are made, project planners must begin to think about recruiting personnel, implementing service delivery, developing an information system, putting in place the budget and accounting procedures, and clarifying the methods of program evaluation and accountability.

Staff Recruitment: A number of personnel are necessary to operate a disaster project, including both professional and nonprofessional workers and clerical assistants. The program plan should detail the number of staff required for the project and should include a description of their assigned duties. It is helpful to have expected activities stated in a job description.

In hiring a project director, mental health administrators and/or members of the task force should look for the following characteristics:
- Administrative experience and ability to make decisions, handle budgets, write reports, and analyze data;
- Intimate knowledge of the community and its resources;
- Skill in mobilizing community groups and resources for action;
- Skill in clinical work, with ability to train and supervise staff; and
- Ability to get along and communicate with a variety of people.

This person should be able to instill confidence in others, provide leadership, be well organized, and take the initiative in solving problems.

The individuals who deliver direct service to disaster victims may be professional or nonprofessional, depending on the financial resources and the availability of manpower in the community. In most instances, some trained clinicians skilled in crisis intervention, group treatment modalities, and outreach work should be sought as supervisors, center directors, or trainers. In some instances, nonprofessionals might be recruited to locate victims in need of service and to provide supportive short-term counseling. Administrators should try to recruit people from the affected area and should look for the following in their professional and nonprofessional staffs:
- Intimate knowledge of the community and its resources;

- Ability to relate well with others;
- Skill or potential skill in offering counseling assistance to victims; and
- Demonstrated maturity, motivation, and stability.

These potential workers should also reflect the ethnic, racial, class, and religious composition of the community. The process of recruitment may be both formal and informal. Administrators can advertise in local newspapers, send announcements to community agencies and universities, and contact professional societies in their formal recruitment efforts. They may also talk with agency directors, community and civic leaders, and various professionals and nonprofessionals in order to make job possibilities known. Because there is limited time to recruit staff before initiating the project, these steps may be started as funding is sought.

Service Delivery Models: Delivery of assistance to disaster victims requires clarity in organizing help, dividing labor, and delegating authority. Decentralized programs often have centers located in the affected neighborhoods, with a team assigned the responsibility of servicing that area. In these cases, a member serves as administrator and supervisor of team activities and also reports to the project's director. Other projects with a more centralized structure may have only one facility but may assign teams the responsibility of doing outreach work and crisis counseling within a particular geographical area. Both types should address the question of who is to do what and who is responsible to whom. Obviously these choices depend upon the abilities of staff, their interests, and the needs of the program.

In Managua, for example, the disaster team's home and headquarters was one of the few undamaged houses located on the edge of the destroyed area. Each morning all the project workers would meet there to set goals and strategies for the day. After working in the various makeshift clinics, they would return to headquarters at night to share information, evaluate their work, and discuss problems in delivering service. These discussions resulted in modifying and reinforcing the organizational structures of the project. In addition, representatives of other agencies often attended the evening meetings. This served to orient others to the work of the teams and also produced an opportunity to discuss cooperative arrangements.

Information System: Each program requires a system for keeping records and collecting information. The project director must manage the monies granted to the project by setting up accounting and book-keeping procedures so as to have accurate records of funds allocated for space, equipment, materials, supplies, and the payment of staff. Records are also required of workers to note the progress of clients; these case forms must be carefully maintained to ensure confidentiality. The forms note the workers' observations, actions, and progress in helping individuals and families and are frequently used in meetings with supervisors. The project must also collect information on its clients and the type of service being provided. This statistical form might include the following information:

- Demographic information in victims, i.e., age, sex, marital status, education, occupation, income, and number of dependents;
- Disaster-related data, such as degree of loss suffered and physical and emotional symptoms;
- Historical information about other problems, prior mental health status, degrees of preexisting stress, and support systems; and
- Treatment data, such as number of visits, type of help, and treatment outcome.

As part of implementing the program, the project director must design the necessary forms for budgeting and accounting, for case management, and for maintaining required statistical information on the project. For instance, the federally funded disaster project in Massachusetts developed an elaborate management information system for the purpose of keeping records, developing trends, and reporting to internal and external sources. Key aspects of the system consisted of strict procedures for the security, confidentiality, and orderly maintenance of files. From records that included a client-case form, a log of staff activities, a team report, and centralized financial and budget forms, the project generated reports to NIMH, the Federal Coordinating Officer (FCO), and the State Coordinating Officer (SCO) of FEMA. In addition, internal reports were prepared for the project's task force and the Commissioner of Mental Health.

Evaluation and Accountability: As the project progresses, there is a need to evaluate individual and collective performances and to report to authorities on program activities. By reviewing statistical forms, authorities will have an understanding of each worker's activities and will have a view of victims and their problems. The data may be used to make reassignments or to alter program strategies. In addition, this information may be aggregated on a regular basis for the purpose of providing the task force, community leaders, and the funding source with a report of project activities. As these reports are frequently required by the funding agency, the statistical data on the project can be used to meet the requirements of accountability.

In review, this chapter presents a model for the planning and administration of a mental health program for disaster victims. Description of the planning process includes the steps necessary to obtain sanction, assess need, survey resources, set goals, consider alternatives, and design a program. The issues of funding, administrative structures, staff recruitment, service delivery strategies, information systems, evaluation, and accountability are also set forth as dimensions applied to the implementation and administration of a project.

5

EDUCATION AND CONSULTATION

Two of the principal components of any disaster project are education and consultation. Once the project has been planned, administrators and practitioners must turn their attention to problem solving when the community, the care-giving agencies, and their own staff present a lack of knowledge, skill and confidence. Through educational and consultation activities, mental health professionals not only disseminate information and problem-solving skills, but also create a positive environment of support for the disaster program.

Educational activities generally include two elements, education of the public and training and orientation of disaster workers. The targets of these educational activities are the community at large; civic, social, or political groups in the area; human service and disaster relief agencies; and the staff of the mental health program. This presentation assumes that a disaster has occurred, but it is also important to keep in mind the usefulness of these educational elements as a means to orient the general public and mental health professionals in communities that are disaster prone. Predisaster education in the area of mental health is an important aspect of the total preparedness of a community.

Consultation, a key activity of community psychiatry, is also a cornerstone of any postdisaster mental health project. Consultation is the professional activity of a disaster program that is designed to promote the incorporation of mental health procedures into disaster assistance approaches. Specifically, its purpose is the early identification and use of human resources to alleviate the disastrous effects of traumatic experiences among disaster victims. As a method of problem solving, consultation generally addresses the issues at the case and program levels in order to achieve these purposes.

To implement educational and consultative activities, mental health workers must be sensitive to a number of issues. These include sanction, relationship, definition and boundaries of the problem, and professional trust. As professionals, these workers must have an intimate knowledge of the community and must also have established contacts that allow them a point of entry. With the proper identification of key decision makers, sanction is readily gotten and maintained. Without this sanction, the chances of success are limited. Both education and consultation depend upon the development of relationships that define the mature boundaries of the problem and the role of the mental health professional in disaster assistance programs. Trust is gained by listening to others as they define their problems, creating an atmosphere of working collaboratively, demonstrating competence, and always maintaining confidentiality.

This chapter presents some of the dimensions of educational and consultation activities for a mental health program for disaster victims. The main purpose of these activities is to provide knowledge, sharpen skills, instill confidence, foster collaboration, and create support for a mental health effort following a natural catastrophe.

EDUCATION

In the implementation of educational activities, mental health specialists must have skill in community organization, communications (both verbal and written), treatment interventions, and supervision. Perhaps, the most needed skill is that of teacher—the ability to impart to others the knowledge, methods or confidence for understanding disaster behavior and for the psychological assistance of calamity victims. This section discusses the requirements for public relations and for the orientation and training of disaster workers.

Public Education

The purposes of a public education campaign associated with the project are threefold:
- To gain widespread support for the program;
- To publicize services; and
- To report to the community on the program's activities and progress.

Community sanction and support are necessary for the effective planning and implementation of a mental health project for disaster victims, and without these the program may experience difficulties associated with lack of support or low visibility. When a program begins, public information about the project's activities and location is essential. This type of publicity may take several forms:
- It may educate the public to the fact that certain physical and emotional discomfort following a calamity are normal reactions to stress;
- If there is a need for help, victims may seek assistance from the project by calling or visiting its office; and

- The general public has a right to know about the activities and progress of the mental health project.

For example:

The Managuan mental health project was on the verge of collapse due to the publication of a team member's criticism of the government when the second U.S. team arrived in May 1973. One of the new arrivals, a psychologist who was also an expert in media communications, decided to develop a campaign to save the project. Through an appearance on a popular TV program and subsequent articles in the local newspapers, this person conveyed the message that it is normal to feel anxious and sad when one has experienced great loss from an earthquake. The psychologist's theme was that Managuans were, in effect, heroes, a theme that was repeated for some time by the media.

The result of this media message was (1) to publicize the availability of service to those who felt they needed to talk with someone; (2) to convey the message that is was acceptable to feel strong emotions of loss; and (3) to reestablish support for the project. For the team members, this was a turning point.

Public education must begin immediately after the disaster strikes and should continue until the project terminates. The emphasis of the effort varies over time. Getting support is usually the first priority, followed by public education and then reporting to the community.

All types of media can be employed during the public relations campaign. Local newspapers usually publish information on community services. This may be encouraged by writing press releases and inviting reporters to project meetings or activities. Local radio and television stations also have time available for community programming. These programs may include talk shows, reports, or specialized formats, such as health information or community concerns. Arrangements to use the media require some knowledge of reporting requirements and providing information to the appropriate reporter, program director, or responsible person.

Project personnel may also develop a speaker's bureau to educate certain groups in the community, such as politicians; teachers; religious, civic, or social leaders; or directors of human service organizations. A developed presentation, including video materials, slides, or graphics, will aid education objectives and will, in some instances, encourage collaboration among services. For example:

The Massachusetts mental health program, Project Concern, received many requests from the public media and other disaster agencies for information about the psychological consequences of the blizzard and flood. Although staff appeared on television and radio talk programs, it was impossible to meet the many requests of civic and social groups for information. At that point, a video tape on human behavior in the wake of disaster and on the crisis intervention techniques was suggested. With the participation of mental health workers, Red Cross volunteers, and a graduate school of nursing, Project Concern and three disaster experts prepared a one-hour video tape. The local branch of the University of Massachusetts donated video facilities and specialists to make the film.

Copies of the tape were widely distributed to local mental health clinics, the Red Cross, the federal disaster agency, and universities. The actual collaboration of various groups in making the film, as well as the hundreds who relived it, contributed to a greater understanding of disaster reaction, awareness of the mental health project, and the support rendered the program.

Orientation and Training of Project Staff

A number of objectives have been formulated to meet the needs of project personnel and volunteers for knowledge, skill, and orientation. Usually, training goals include the following:

- Knowledge of disaster behavior;
- Skill in the use of treatment modalities;
- Understanding the system of disaster aid;
- Esprit de corps; and
- Supervision.

To accomplish these training objectives, mental health administrators must design short- and long-term programs for professionals and nonprofessionals. In the immediate aftermath of a catastrophe, both mental health and relief workers need a quick, flexible orientation. There is seldom sufficient time to plan these training sessions, which are generally put together on the spur of the moment. Later on, a more planned effort to provide continued training and support for the project's professional and nonprofessional staff must be devised. Training content will vary depending upon the experience, specific needs, and educational background of the trainees.

Disaster Behavior: The primary training need is knowledge and understanding of how disaster victims react after a mishap. By reviewing the time phases of disaster (preimpact, impact, and postimpact) participants can examine the types of physical and emotional problems victims can be expected to suffer at each phase. Although the study of victims' emotional behavior following a calamity is in its infancy, there are enough information and research findings to orient workers.

Included in the study of victims' symptoms are concepts related to understanding and diagnosing their problems. Training in the concepts of crisis/stress, loss and mourning, systems of social and emotional support, and coping/adaptation are crucial in gaining mastery of disaster problems.

Treatment Skills: Another goal of training is presenting ways to help victims in distress. Depending on the knowledge and skill trainees already have, trainers may wish to focus on such techniques as:

- Crisis counseling;
- Group therapy for adults;
- Play therapy for children;
- Family group therapy; and
- Short-term focus therapy.

Trainees also need to know about outreach, advocacy, and community organization. Because disaster victims seldom seek service from a mental health clinic, project workers must acquire techniques for entering the community in search of victims. In an outreach model, individuals are located outside the project's office and treatment is frequently provided under nontraditional circumstances. Skill in community organization prepares the project workers to mobilize citizen support, work with communities, and organize agency resources to aid both the project and the victims.

Disaster Aid System: Disaster victims who present emotional problems also have a variety of real needs that must be resolved, such as needs for shelter, medical care, home repairs, and financial assistance. Mental health workers thus need a thorough knowledge of the community's resources. Because these resources vary from community to community, a trainee must understand the local system of health and human services, as well as the range of relief services provided by private and public organizations at the local, state, and federal levels. Mental health workers will need knowledge of the services offered, the criteria for getting those services, and methods for referring clients.

Esprit de Corps: High staff morale depends upon the clarity of project goals and the importance of purpose. Because it is essential for effective operation of the mental health project, another purpose of training is building and maintaining the staff's esprit de corps.

Low staff morale results from several factors, including lack of support, lack of skill in doing a job, and job pressures. Workers need to talk about their work-related problems and need visible support and reassurance from the project's authorities. Staff who are poorly equipped to assist victims will react with frustration, guilt, and anger. Probably one of the most serious problems of mental health workers in disaster assistance is overwork leading to fatigue and withdrawal. This is especially grave in the first days after the disaster because workers toil long hours under stress and chaos. The outcome of these conditions is frequently a "burnt-out" feeling and a lowering of morale.

Training programs should address these potential problems directly by incorporating time during the sessions to discuss and share problems and feelings. Social activities from time to time also serve to maintain group sentiment, dispel frustration, and lead to more effective work.

Supervision: Major tasks of supervision include continued orientation and training of staff, effective delivery of service to victims, support of project workers, and overall integration of the project. The program's personnel should continue to learn by reviewing with the supervisor knowledge areas and techniques that are useful to performing the job. This educational component is an integral part of the supervisory process.

Workers will also need consultation and assistance in dealing with their clients' problems. Although related to the educational component, this supervisory step is problem-focused, so that staff members can apply knowledge and techniques to each victim's situation. Project staff are often tired, overworked, and frustrated, due to the long hours and pressures of their activities. Supervision must therefore address the staff need for sharing, reassurance, and support. Maintenance of staff morale is facilitated by the supervisor and includes the important process of terminating when the project ends.

It is also necessary for all project members to follow certain established procedures. The administrative requirements of the project, which include standards of service, the need for information, and contacts with other agencies, lend the program an overall consistency and integration. Therefore, the administrative element is also a goal of supervision.

Supervisors have various techniques in their work. The more traditional approach includes regular meetings between worker and supervisor to cover educational, problem-solving, morale, and administrative issues. Other supervisors may prefer to cover these issues in small groups, relying upon the dynamics and interactions of workers to enhance the supervisory process. Often these approaches may be combined for maximum effect.

Training Tools: Several things are important to remember when carrying out training activities. Training, including supervision, is a process that begins on the first day of the project and ends when the program closes. Training activities during this time must be planned so that learning objectives are sequenced and consistent. The plan for training and supervision should include a published schedule of dates and times of meetings so that all will know about them. One procedure is to have a set date for these activities and to announce in advance the topics for presentation or discussion. Trainers and supervisors must also put together all types of materials, including video tapes, slides, movies, and case materials for use during training sessions. The training format may include didactic presentations, discussions, problem solving, and role playing. It is commonly believed that techniques which enhance involvement and sharing are effective tools in learning. The trainers chosen may be project participants, consultants, local agency or university personnel, or speakers who have specific knowledge about a service or about behavioral reactions or intervention.

CONSULTATION

Mental health consultation is one of the essential ingredients of an organized intervention program following a community disaster. Members of the mental health consultation organization must articulate a plan that harmonizes with all the other elements of the disaster-assisting agencies. The main mission of all these agencies is to support and concretely reorganize the lives of the citizens affected. A mental health consultant working in a temporary shelter or a one-stop federal center is more than an independent professional responding only to the necessity of aiding the victims. S/he must also help other agency staff deal with upset individuals by using skills appropriate for mental health workers. The consultant must place him/herself within a dynamic interplay of social system factors that are continually being modified by the situation in the postdisaster area. Each helping agency there will have specific goals and relative priorities, according to the most pressing needs of the population, the supply of resources, and the availability of other assisting services. All these factors must be carefully coordinated to reach a large number of victims with effective and efficient approaches because needs usually exceed resources.

There is a need to develop an appropriate set of conceptual models in order to provide the mental health staff with the guidelines and the language to develop the consultation program. Consultation is one method the mental health professional can use to facilitate the work of other professionals helping the population in the disaster area. The first steps in the process of consultation include creating proximity and establishing a relationship that allows for the opportunity to demonstrate competence and eagerness to help, while at the same time respecting the right of other agencies to develop their tasks and functions. After achieving this basic goal by offering collaborative co-professional services for the victims, mental health workers must begin to understand the operations of their counterparts in the other agencies and to formulate ways they can assist. This will sometimes mean accepting the "referred case" without delay or questions about whether or not the case is suitable for psychological assistance. This stage is followed by a rapid development of communications changes, which involve identifying the key members of the assisting networks who have access to the significant groups of line workers, as well as to the authority system at the affected site. Mental health consultants then must work out the terms of the consulting arrangements so that agency needs will be communicated to the consultant, who can then respond rapidly.

There are two types of obstacles to free communication between the consultant and agency personnel. The first type emanates from realistic conflicts of interest. This requires compromises in the development of a common language to clarify objectives, guidelines, and tasks. The second type of obstacle results from distorted perceptions or unrealistic expectations. Thus agency staff may view the consultant as either "all knowing" or "ignorant and irrelevant." In either case, these issues must be resolved before proceeding with the consultation.

Conflicts between consultants and staff of the problem-solving agency can easily occur. For example, it may be possible that Red Cross workers have developed a variety of ways to deal with victims' problems over the years. Each of these workers will have his or her own method of approaching a problem. Each may feel, with specific emotional reactions, that a mental health consultant may be ignorant of issues of assistance, may influence the process, and may change the methodology of operations. Methodology developed over a long period of time by the Red Cross worker can be threatened when different approaches seem more efficient. Workers may also be threatened if someone helps them do a better job; this sets up an ambivalent reaction of both gratefulness and distrust or fear of being found inept. Until the consultant finds out what each worker has been doing and carefully defines a role which does not overlap that domain, and unless the consultant succeeds in communicating this clearly, other workers may overtly or covertly oppose entry into their system. The consultant needs to look at the following tasks and rapidly find ways to accomplish them:

- Dealing with any distorted perceptions and expectations of the agency workers;
- Developing trust and respect;
- Developing both verbal and nonverbal communications;
- Ensuring grounds for collaboration; and
- Designing successive stages of roles, according to the phases of the disaster.

Following is an example of developing the consultation model in the first phase. The mental health consultant will be regularly assigned for service in the shelter during a certain period of time. This consultant may be from any of the mental health disciplines, that is, a psychiatrist, psychologist, social worker, or psychiatric nurse. He or she will attend to any situation the agency staff wishes to discuss in relation to mental health issues presented by victims. For example, a consultee might wish to clarify his understanding of symptoms observed in a victim. The worker's approach to the problem may be devised on the basis of information or comments from the consultant. However, the consultant should not make any direct suggestions for choice or action. If workers need to reach a decision on what to do in the face of alternatives, their supervisor should guide them according to customary agency policy.

The content of all discussions with a consultant is geared to the situation of the victim and not to the feelings of the disaster assistance worker or his own life experiences. It is taken for granted that the worker is concerned about certain perplexing or unclear aspects of the victim's situation, and the consultation will be limited to this area. The worker's own feelings, important as they may be, are considered inappropriate for discussion. Neither is it considered appropriate to analyze any possible reasons for differences of opinion between staff workers or between staff and supervisors. A worker who wants to meet with a consultant should ask a supervisor to find one in the shelter or to contact a consultant in the specific area of crisis counseling. The following case study is illustrative:

The director of the community supports agency, one of the disaster relief agencies in a town devastated by a tornado, asked for consultation because his staff was showing emotional strain and fatigue. At the time of the request, the area affected by the tornado was still in shambles; houses had been destroyed and rubble littered every square foot. The affected population had been relocated to a college dormitory, and agency staff were serving the victims in all types of daily living, housing, food, and recreation needs. They had been working around the clock for ten days. Town policies, enforced by the mayor, did not allow flexibility to change some of the procedures that would offer relief and better schedules for the workers. The agency director was urged by one of his staff to seek consultation in dealing with the problems.

The director and his staff met with the consultant and, at their first meeting, outlined the problems as decreased energy and increased staff frustration due to continuous and increased complaints by the victims. The major complaint was that people had no privacy, everything was too structured, and nothing was working because little individual or group help was available. This problem was most acute when dealing with the displaced adolescents. Efforts to involve the parents in looking at this problem (involving for example, vandalism to the college property) and efforts to find solutions were not effective.

When the administrator turned to the consultant for a possible solution, the consultant raised the issue of needing specific data on how the families were grouped in the dormitory, how the day was organized, how the staff was dealing with the problems, and how the recipients of all this help felt about the effort. It was suggested that some of the data could be gathered by the consultant in small group meetings at the college dormitory, but the consultant wanted the staff members to participate, too. This last idea was resisted because the staff felt that they had enough to do and because they were ambivalent about reviewing their own behavior and procedures. After more clarification of how important the data gathering would be in finding ways to alleviate the load of the workers, some volunteers met with the consultant. In this meeting, it became clear that most of the staff were tired and angry over servicing victims who were seen as ungrateful, manipulative, selfish, and greedy. They were also disturbed because they did not know how long the families would stay before they could return to some temporary housing.

Several areas were delineated for further fact finding. First, which were the most difficult families? Second, what were their losses and how capable were they in planning for the future? Third, what type of things seemed to bring out the most irritation and anger in these families? Fourth, what could be helpful in making staff members feel more relaxed and capable? The staff undertook the task of finding data to answer these questions. They were also asked to note any procedures that were especially effective in handling the problems faced in helping the victims. It was hoped that this information might provide insight for further discussion.

Two days later the staff presented their findings, and it became clear that many approaches of the staff signaled their own frustrations. As a result of the mass of data gathered, a number of ideas about effecting change in routine and approaches were brought forth. With the support of the consultant and agreement of the administrator, several changes in schedules, procedures, and duties were tried. These changes reflected a more realistic way to run the agency. A stronger link with Red Cross volunteers and crisis counselors was also established. The volunteers developed recreation plans for the adolescents, and the crisis counselors had small group meetings with the parents. Discussion focused on how the crisis in their lives had disrupted their routines and exasperated them. They were thus able to ventilate many emotional issues. At the same time, the victims were asked to suggest ways they could work with the agency staff.

All this material was gathered by the consultant, who in turn helped the staff see their stereotyped reactions to the victims and realistically understand the victims' plight and reactions to their losses. With enhanced communication between the groups, the assistance program, which lasted two more weeks, became a more satisfying and less harassing experience for the agency.

Victim-Centered Case Consultation

Victim-centered case consultation is the type most often needed in a disaster center. Disaster workers often have difficulty dealing with the mental health problems presented by victims and can use the assistance and advice of mental health workers. Usually the relief worker will present the problem to the mental health professional, but at times the latter can also examine the victim, reach a diagnostic impression, and make recommendations. The agency worker can then translate appropriate aspects of the recommendations into a plan that seems feasible in the shelter or other disaster assistance setting.

The primary task of this type of consultation is to develop a plan that will help the victim. When the mental health consultant intervenes to help a specific victim, it is assumed that this victim has difficulties of an unusual nature and that very few other victims will have the same difficulties or will need a similar approach to resolve them. In most cases, the mental health consultant will personally investigate the victim's needs. In this way, the agency workers gain an increasing awareness and understanding of certain aspects of the case through discussion with the consultant. The mental health professional will try to obtain accurate, specific, and reliable information on the victim and may then come to a conclusion and offer diagnostic recommendations. The prescription for disposition and management of the case should be clear, acceptable, and feasible to the agency worker, who will then be responsible for taking action. Cases and approaches vary through the various phases of a disaster program. Following is an example:

A Red Cross worker asked for consultation on Mr. S., a displaced teacher living in a motel room. He had been exhibiting disruptive behavior, and had been constantly intruding into groups assembled in the sitting areas of the motel, where part of the displaced population had been housed after a flood. At the initial meeting, the mental health worker noted an edge of hostility as the Red Cross worker described Mr. S.'s behavior and his refusal to accept any controls. As the consultant sympathized with the problem of controlling Mr. S.'s behavior, the Red Cross worker felt supported and was able to present both Mr. S.'s problems and her own frustration. The consultant suggested that data on Mr. S.'s previous life and the effects of the disaster on him be obtained. The Red Cross worker commented that she had met with Mr. S. several times to discuss his numerous problems, which included the loss of three other teaching jobs due to occasional alcohol abuse.

The consultant told the worker that he had had experience with Mr. S.'s types of problems, thereby implying that she might want to share the responsibility of taking care of Mr. S. with another professional. He also assured her that the behavior manifested by Mr. S. was not due to a lack of professional knowledge on her part. The consultant promised to meet with the worker a couple of times a week after he interviewed Mr. S. so that both could consider how Mr. S.'s emotional problems were related to his uncontrollable behavior. Together they could decide on the best method to help Mr. S.

An interview with Mr. S. revealed helpful information. He told about his lonely life as a 47-year-old bachelor with few friends. He said that his family lived in another state, and that he lost his teaching job in a nearby school when it closed after the disaster. He generally was shy, quiet, and worried about people talking about him. To lower his anxiety and boredom, he often drank in excess and had been expelled from two previous positions because of his drinking. Having to leave his apartment, live and sleep in a shelter with no privacy, and then stay in a motel with no possibility of leaving because of the flooding waters had unleashed intense anger in him and he could not control his irritability. He had very few social skills to adapt to group living.

The consultant met again with the Red Cross worker and made clear that

Mr. S.'s aggressive and negative behavior had a long history but had been well defended by isolation and work habits. In the motel setting, however, this man had few defenses to deal with his feelings. The consultant suggested to the worker ways in which she could intervene to help Mr. S. structure his routine in a more satisfactory way, which in turn would strengthen his usual defenses and lower his obnoxious behavior. The worker smiled and her face brightened as she remarked, "Yes, these are difficult times for all of us."

Program-Centered Consultation

Another type of consultation focuses on the orientation or modification of program structures and administrative procedures for the purpose of prevention, early diagnosis and treatment, and rehabilitation of disaster-related mental disturbances. Mental health intervention following a natural calamity is one of the components in a system of help and support for victims. Other programs, such as the Red Cross, Family Service, welfare department, church agencies, and local mental health clinics, may wish to develop a specialized service for disaster refugees.

Leaders in adjacent areas impacted by the catastrophe may also desire to set up a crisis intervention and counseling project for their affected population. In either instance, an expert mental health professional may provide consultation centered upon the design or modification of a program to provide psychological assistance to victims as part of the overall package.

The type of problems addressed by the consultant are varied, but will probably include such issues as:

- Program planning;
- Appropriate administrative structures;
- Methods of service delivery;
- Policy setting;
- Recruitment, training, and utilization of staff; and
- Establishment of linkages with other human services.

The recipient of the consultation may be an administrator, a group of program directors, or a committee, such as a task force or board of directors. The consultant's focus could be either a program in question or the consultee's abilities to master problems in planning and administration of a project.

These two types of consultation, victim-centered and program-centered, involve an intervention between the mental health expert (consultant) and the person dealing with a task that presents a problem (consultee). In all instances, the consultant is presumed to have the knowledge to help resolve the problem now and in the future, while the consultee always maintains responsibility for the case or the program. The role of the consultant is to examine goals, methods, and techniques in order to overcome a lack of knowledge, skill, and/or confidence. In using this problem-solving method, the consultant employs many aspects of his role, including teaching, analyzing, planning, coordinating, collaborating, negotiating, or counseling. In all instances, the consultant is concerned with promoting the incorporation of mental health components in communities devastated by disaster. Those components should be designed to help organize the lives of victims and ensure the early detection and prompt treatment of those who suffer psychological consequences from the calamity.

6

POSTDISASTER
PSYCHOLOGICAL INTERVENTION

The mental health professional generally begins direct face-to-face intervention with populations housed in emergency shelters. Large numbers of individuals are relocated following the damage to their homes and neighborhoods. Professionals at such relocation centers have at their disposal the knowledge and skills to offer psychological help to a gathered group of victims in need.

This chapter will identify and organize a number of approaches devoloped to assist victims through the phases of crisis, coping, and adaptation. A group of techniques appropriate to the initial postdisaster period will be described under the rubrics of triage and first-aid auxiliary assistance. As individuals move through their changing concrete world and their psychophysiological phases of crisis resolution, interventive therapeutic procedures are indicated and will be described. In the subsequent phases, the activities of the professional will resemble and incorporate many of the approaches and procedures of crisis counseling, short-term therapy, comprehensive support, and long-term therapy.

OBJECTIVES

A major objective of mental health disaster intervention is the successful use of techniques that (1) restore the capacity of victims to handle the stressful situations in which they find themselves, and (2) help them reorder and organize their world through social interaction. Mental health workers provide education about and interpretation of the overwhelming emotions experienced by disaster victims in order to help those victims understand the reactive nature of their feelings and recover a sense of capability and hopefulness. In short, the skills of the mental health worker are used to offer assistance and support to a stressed population.

A second objective of mental health disaster intervention is active, continued collaboration with other support and care-giving groups and with the agencies assisting both the victim and the community. The acceptance of mental health workers as collaborators by disaster assistance groups is a relatively new phenomenon, and the appropriate procedures for fostering this acceptance have been described earlier. Although this chapter deals exclusively with face-to-face intervention, the mental health worker continually needs to be aware of disaster agency staff behavior and objectives. These influence the crisis resolution of the victim, which is the main focus of mental health workers' efforts.

CONCEPTS

To achieve this aim of crisis resolution, mental health workers must single out concepts within their professional knowledge in the following areas:

Role

The professional must accept a team member role of participating rapidly and effectively as the human problems appear. He or she must be aware of major influences in the living conditions of the victim, which are beyond the professional's capacity to change along major parameters, while still accepting the responsibility to indicate, educate, influence, and (if an M.D.) prescribe medication. All efforts should be directed toward a helpful role for both victims and the caretakers. This direction must be coupled with a sense of empathy and a sensitivity to the tragic events associated with the disaster.

Techniques

Several techniques are available to the professional to assist in crisis resolution; they can be grouped under the heading of "ego auxiliary techniques." These approaches are directed toward restoring ego functions and can be instrumental in reintegrating and returning to balance the total ego system.

Techniques within this psychotherapeutic approach are defined as *any active interaction that tends to supplement, complement, reinforce, or promote ego mechanisms in the victim*. In restoring the function of adaptive mechanisms, drug therapy may be indicated, depending upon knowledge of its therapeutic effects and the indicated usage according to diagnostic categories.

Process

The range of procedures (behavior, action, speech, types of meetings, face-to-face interaction) through which process occurs will depend on the situation encountered by the professional. The victim's situation, the manifestation of the crisis in psychophysiologic signs and symptoms, and the resources available to assist this individual will influence the procedures available to the mental health professional to achieve the objectives of intervention. This is a major reason why psychological disaster assistance varies so much from psychological assistance provided in a clinic or hospital. There the professional is in control of many of the conditions of that concrete clinical world; in the shelters or transitional housing accommodations, conditions are generally complex and unpredictable. This added role shift required of mental health professionals adds to the burden of providing postdisaster help.

Level of Responsibility

This area of professional behavior is singled out here for emphasis. Although this might be considered as part of role definition, it should be highlighted as a major contribution to mental health therapeutic intervention. There is a wide range of personal choices available to the professional for taking responsibility and *actively* participating in disaster assistance. These options can be exemplified by, on one end of the spectrum, the professional who climbs into a helicopter with the Red Cross workers hours after the disaster and, on the other end of the spectrum, by the professional who sits at a desk in the shelter or waits in the mental health clinic for individuals to show up with signs of emotional disturbance asking for help. All these activities can be effective and helpful in varying degrees and depend upon professional philosophy, the availability of professionals, and the circumstances of the disaster.

Therapeutic Objectives

Therapeutic crisis intervention encompasses all the activities by which the professional seeks to relieve the distress and modify the behavior of the victim through psychological means. It encompasses all helping activities based on communication that is primarily, although not necessarily, based on words. Many of these traumatized individuals display a sense of hopelessness and demoralization. All forms of therapy use certain approaches to combat and control this painful effect. Demoralized victims show behavior that reflects the feeling of being unable to cope with the multiple problems that they and others expect them to handle. This state of mind can vary widely in duration and severity, but the following manifestations are often found among the victims:

- They express feelings of diminished self-confidence and cannot remember past ability to master traumatic episodes. They are overwhelmed not only by the postdisaster external circumstances, but by their own confusing feelings and thoughts in reaction to their new, uncomfortable, and unfamiliar world;
- The consequent belief that failure will be the outcome of all their decisions and actions serves to strengthen feelings of guilt and shame as part of the adaptive regression;
- The victims typically feel alienated, depressed, and isolated, as if they had been singled out, even though they see others "in the same boat";
- The victims may also have feelings of resentment because others whom they count on for help seem unable or unwilling to do so. The behavior of those others, in turn, may realistically express irritation because of their unconscious expectations of the victim and their feelings of entitlement as part of their own fatigue and frustration. This often creates a vicious circle between victims, families, and agency workers; and
- Because of increased dependency on others, there is a lack of feedback that builds the person's self-esteem and further distance is created. Occasionally there is a loss of faith in group values and in former beliefs of peers that had, in the past, given the victim a sense of security and significance in the world, and this faith needs reordering. This accounts for occasional looting as an outcome behavior. Such behavior is especially evident when the disaster has occurred in a major urban setting where the authorities and governmental bodies have been fragmented, and where some groups appear to profit from the disaster through vandalism and theft, at the expense of the victims.

The points just listed should serve to clarify the objectives behind the activities of the mental health worker. The purpose of such activities is to intervene in order to bring about a change in the victims' problem-solving capabilities, which have been weakened by the disaster conditions. Mental health workers may also take appropriate action working directly with the victims and with agency staff to assure that the individuals no longer regard themselves as being in a helpless and hopeless crisis position.

The main objectives of psychological processes with disaster victims are:

- To help victims develop an internal sense of order and perspective, so they will be able to organize their own environments as they are helped to process the painful and powerful emotions accompanying the postdisaster events; and

- To intervene and help the victims reach out, acquire, and build upon the resources they have received from the assisting recovery agencies directly within the environment, so that, through the proper use of these resources, victims will gain real help in reordering their world, and in that process, will develop a sense of comfort, security, and self-esteem.

In sum, mental health workers mobilize available resources to help victims reorder their environment and alleviate emotional conflict and physical discomfort. This process of intervention therefore includes planning and providing victims with access to and use of these resources.

GUIDELINES FOR INTERVENTION

Intervention procedures are related to assessment, problem solving, and decision making. Mental health workers should look at the following guidelines in order to plan the appropriate type and level of activity. Interventions must be planned in terms of immediacy versus service objectives and should depend upon the phase of the disaster and upon living conditions.

Risk Factors

The level of psychobiological status of the victim is related to the vulnerability of the personality and to one's biological state. For example, high anxiety, depression, cardiac pain, high blood pressure, and disturbance of gastric functions are not uncommon among disaster victims. To be able to measure all this, mental health practitioners must investigate the following:

- The psychosocial maturity or immaturity of a victim's personality;
- Role stress or social expectations of performance, as judged by the victims and others living with them;
- Continued environmental stress, both in social and physical accommodations; and
- Accidental crisis events occurring in the victims' lives either before or after the disaster.

Social Setting

The setting where the victim is located is an important variable that will affect the choice of psychological intervention. This is based on the experience of assisting victims in crowded shelter settings. The rapid turnover of large numbers of victims in and out of the shelter and the small number of trained staff who stay for long periods of time with victims mold the types of intervention. The question is, what can be useful within the specific setting with the specific professional resources available?

Use of Medical and Clinical Resources

The diagnosis of serious threat to life needs prompt assistance from medical colleagues and should be part of the evaluation process. Persons with a history of drug or alcohol abuse who are experiencing difficulty in their functioning may require heroic efforts to secure transportation to the nearest hospital.

UNDERLYING PRINCIPLES SUPPORTING GUIDELINES

There is a need to prepare the individual for this type of postdisaster crisis counseling and psychological intervention. The crisis counselor accomplishes this by obtaining the information needed to plan the intervention, by establishing competence and credibility in the victim's eyes, by describing the intervention plan, and by eliciting the victim's cooperation with the plan. The plan must analyze the individual's attitudes and expectations about the intervention and then move forward to a collaborative plan. From this analysis, the crisis counselor arrives at a tentative formulation of the problem and/or the plan of action.

Crisis counselors should be familiar with a wide variety of approaches and should master those that best suit their personal styles. Within this range, the combination that best fits the characteristics of the problem should be chosen. The therapeutic objectives are to alleviate emotional distress and/or cognitive disorganization and to offer the patient corrective experiences and information. Crisis counselors are primary agents to achieve this objective, but their effectiveness can often be increased by including other helpers.

The following key principles should be recognized:

- Crisis counselors should assume that victims are potentially capable of handling their own problems after being helped to recognize barriers to solutions or to redirect their behavior toward exploring new solutions;
- Counselors should discourage dependence upon them, although they may let it develop initially so that victims can borrow confidence from the counselors;
- Advice should generally be given with caution, although this does not preclude informing victims about all relevant matters on which they are ignorant or misinformed. This helps to enhance the problem-solving capability of victims;
- Communication in the initial interview may be difficult because victims often have distorted ways of communicating, due to high

anxiety and cognitive disorganization. Often they are also some-what defensive and guarded. The crisis counselor's success in achieving free communication depends primarily on a general ability to win the victim's trust and confidence;

- Crisis intervention focuses on current life problems. Victims need help in resolving the present crisis produced by the disaster. They need to talk about the "here and now." Encouraging them to do so helps establish a relationship. It allows the counselor to offer feedback or options in solving problems and helps the victim to analyze realistically ways of moving toward the solution of problems;

- Some exploration of past methods of problem solving will aid in understanding how victims handle the present situation. Meaning and symbolism, including the victim's psychophysiologic responses to present events, are largely determined by past experiences. Therefore, a partial review of the past may be needed to understand how victims perceive both the problems they face and the options they can accept in terms of their value systems;

- Interpretation that links feelings or behaviors not previously connected by victims may be therapeutic. This allows people to make sense of feelings that are not clear and, by putting those feelings in perspective, enhance their sense of mastery and control; and

- It is helpful to keep reinforcing positive activities and reminding victims of their skills and strengths in handling problems. The counselor must keep in mind the personal skills that are working well and not get focused only on a victim's weaker aspects of problem solving. Whenever there is a possibility of reinterpreting the behavior in terms of strengths rather than weakness, this should be done.

TYPES OF INTERVENTION ACCORDING TO POSTDISASTER PHASES

First Phase

Phenomenologically, the psychological emergencies will require immediate, rapid evaluation of the victim's behavior. A minimum of data will be available for making decisions, and both time and human energy will be limited. The skill and knowledge required to treat the multiple problems for which officials in a shelter request assistance may seem overwhelming.

The emergency situation not only demands a new role for the mental health worker but also implies types of intervention that can be classed under the concept of "triage." "Disaster triage operations" are the procedures used by team members and other mental health workers to assess behavior, gauge the degree and level of crisis, and supply information. This knowledge is provided to the assisting team so that disaster aid planning can alleviate the immediate situation and the psychophysiologic reactions of victims.

Since victims become cognitive and emotionally disorganized for a temporary period of time, the intervention has to attend to these two areas. Procedures must be implemented to increase competence and maintain awareness that the situation generated by the disaster will demand increased individual mobilization of all the ego skills to adapt to a traumatized environment.

Cognitive disorganization will affect the victim's attention and focus, the level of interest and involvement, the ability to stop ruminating and being obsessed about the catastrophe, the learning capacity to absorb information given by relief agency staff, and the recall of skills available to solve problems. Taking these characteristics into consideration, the therapeutic objective should be to help victims minimize the effects of the disorganization and to reinforce their cognitive mastery. The following areas of psychological assistance are useful in dealing with cognitive disorganization:

- Assisting the victims by reinforcing their concrete world, as exemplified by time, space, scheduling, and recognizing practical living arrangements;
- Strengthening conscious awareness of the appropriateness of the victim's social reactions. Many victims believe "they are going crazy" because they observe changes in their social behavior; informing them of the phenomenology of bereavement is useful;
- Helping victims integrate daily events into the reality of the shelter's conditions;
- Helping people identify realistic causal relationships of events and reactions; and
- Supporting the victims' ventilation of fears that their "minds are not working."

Parallel to those types of intervention for cognitive disorganization, the following procedures are useful in dealing with emotional disorganization. The therapist should be able to gauge rapidly the type and the quality of effect predominant through social interaction with the victim. The major effects seen in the initial phase include sadness, fear, and anger. These are manifested in many forms and with a wide range of intensity. Some expressions are pronounced, while some are subdued and defended.

During the triage and first-aid auxiliary assistance stages, these sets of defenses should not be tampered with. They offer a psychological first-level healing which keeps the personality functioning during the acute phase. Although they offer a vulnerable cover-up to the emotions, it is best not to encourage expression of guarded emotions until an appropriate place and time, when the professional can stay with the victim until the process of recuperating some emotional stability is assured.

We have had little experience in the use of triage and first-aid procedures during the first hours of disaster relief. This, coupled with our lack of codified knowledge of behavioral reactions, usually results in a difficult choice of when to employ these procedures.

Intervention objectives for victims living in shelters would include helping them achieve physical comfort, increased cognitive organization, and a sense of emotional control. These approaches will help diminish the victims' sense of helplessness, their indecisive or regressive behavior, and their belief that they lack coping skills. The approaches will help to increase competence, self-esteem, the flexibility to consider alternative solutions to problems and the ability to bear the confusion and mixed communication that is characteristic of this first phase of disaster assistance.

For the first two to three days, mental health workers need to focus aid proceedings on the basis of a diagnosis of the crisis-symptom manifestations of the victims. They must sort out priorities for action, such as helping with the victim's sense of orientation, reinforcing reality testing, developing support and trust, and ascertaining the needs of the victims for resources that can be obtained and provided by other agencies. In addition to developing support systems around victims, there must also be de facto support systems within the victim group in the temporary shelters.

The great array of resources available must be organized to meet the specific needs of the victims. Many of these needs are concrete, but others are psychological. The mental health worker can mobilize appropriate psychological help by observing the way staff from other agencies behave or approach the victims. This requires a special type of technique that allows the mental health workers to elicit directly and personally from the victims, in their own communication style, what they perceive as immediate needs, to interpret this content, and then to collaborate with other agencies in mobilizing the resources so that the victims feel assisted, less helpless, less hopeless, and less destitute. The primary objective of the first phase is to lessen stress.

Second Phase

As the victims are relocated from emergency shelters to temporary lodgings or back to their homes, which may be damaged but safe, a new phenomenology of bereavement and crisis emerges. This necessitates an increasing repertoire of mental health intervention activities, including crisis counseling with the objective of achieving crisis resolution, crisis intervention, and outreach procedures. Crisis intervention is a modality of psychological procedures that incorporates several psycho-social approaches. All these procedures may be used in a variety of settings and can be adapted to change as both agency relocation planning and the situation of the victims evolve. Combinations of all or at least several of the following activities are usually available to mental health professionals.

Outreach procedures are activities undertaken by professionals going out to the living sites of relocated individuals to identify victims, to assess problems, and to develop relations with identified victims. The victim's level of need is assessed and, if the assessment does not reveal decompensation, a message is conveyed that the staff is available at a specific address or phone number when the victim has a psychological need or interest in using resources.

Outreach activities can help achieve some of the following objectives toward assisting disaster victims:

- Education and information about the resources available to help reorganize their lives;
- Help in identifying ambivalent feelings, acknowledging needs, asking for help, and accepting support from a stranger;
- Help in interacting on a cognitive level, assigning priorities to needs, accepting advice on how to obtain resources, and increasing individual capacity to cope with the specific priorities identified;
- The opportunity to become engaged and affiliated (observed crisis phenomenology indicates an increased need for victims to reach out and a higher level of suggestibility from their social surround-ings); and
- A structured method of perceiving specific problems, self-observa-tions, behavior patterns, and powerful emotions through help in understanding, defining, and ordering events in the larger world.

Once these objectives have been accomplished, each categorical problem can be singled out and suggestions can be made for steps to manage them. At the same time, several areas of cognitive, emotional, behavioral, and social reality are put into perspective as a first approxima-tion toward understanding what is happening.

All these activities are preparatory for further work. If the victim accepts the offer of help from the mental health worker, the victim is led naturally into the now-accepted methodologies of crisis counseling and therapy. These can be accomplished in the home settings or in specified nearby locations chosen by the mental health teams.

Any conditions that create barriers to interaction with the victims, such as distance, transportation, bureaucratic forms and regulations, culturally insensitive procedures, or local anomalies will diminish the chances of success of achieving the goals of the mental health worker.

Once a trusting bond is established with the victim, the worker can proceed to obtain further documentation of the issues affecting him or her. A diagnostic assessment should include information in the following categories:

- Characteristics and vital statistics of the client;
- Mental status and previous major crises;
- Historical events during the disaster;
- Effects of the disaster on property or on family members;
- Major preoccupations and identification of priority problems;
- Personality structure and quality of relating to the mental health worker; and
- Types of skills available to the victim to negotiate the environment.

With this type of information, which generally is very sketchy, the worker then proceeds to develop an "assisting plan of action."

Assisting along the cognitive-emotional-behavioral vectors to achieve crisis resolution is one of the most challenging crisis therapy activities open to mental health professionals. Crisis resolution in victims is manifested by a lowering of tension, a return to cognitive organization, the achievement of relative emotional control, the self-observation of appropriate social behavior interactions, and the ability to deal with the negotiable aspects of obtaining available resources to reconstitute their lives.

Third Phase

As the final phases of the recovery operations develop, multiple categories of cases come to the attention of mental health workers. These cases present different needs in the areas of ego vulnerability and decompensation. Many victims with strong ego structures and good support systems decompensate when another major crisis such as a death, divorce, or loss of employment occurs within a short time of the disaster. Many victims with vulnerable defenses who were able to cope for several weeks begin to show signs of exhaustion. They enter a down-spiral phase and display a failure to cope and poor judgment in making decisions; this condition leads to poor outcome of problem resolutions, increased dependency, and angry behavior. Psychophysiologic symptoms reappear, and problems of a social and legal character increase. Adding to the load in this phenomenology is the fact that the post-disaster support systems that spring up with force, enthusiasm, and resources begin to dwindle and many individuals lose the human matrix that was helping them by:

- Providing auxiliary ego figures and help in testing reality;
- Absorbing the expression of negative feelings;
- Assisting, guiding, and pacing their adaptive efforts; and
- Supporting their ability to bear anxiety, thereby preventing the early closure for receiving information that is essential in making

decisions. This support enhances good judgment and reduces impulsive decision making.

The continuation of crisis intervention activities follows a curve with the majority of cases averaging eight to twelve sessions, followed by peaks of various intervention activities along a time frame of a year.

Psychological assistance to postdisaster victims is one of the most challenging and most stressful of professional practices. It not only demands a repertoire of skills to meet needs, but the intensity of the emotional climate in the disaster setting demands from the worker continuous attention and activity aimed at mitigating and managing all kinds of painful expressions due to stress.

The crisis situation engenders an atmosphere of chaos, disorganization, novelty, and trial/error approaches. People talk to almost anyone to relieve the emotional pressure of experienced incidents and events. All of the recounting is tinged with sadness, anger, confusion, and despair. Grim humor sprinkles their conversation and sarcasm covers up many of the stories. The worker faced with the tasks of supporting the victims and problem solving with them will also be struggling with the reality of bureaucratic issues and with a multitude of unanswerable questions. The outreach and advocacy approaches chosen to assist the victims demands a rapid resolution that often conflicts with the usual bureaucratic responses.

Frustration is an emotion that is easily transmitted and is compounded in the climate in which victims and helpers find themselves. It is necessary to help the workers develop an internal signal system to alert them when the "burnt out" syndrome is setting in. Fatigue, irritability, impatience, ambivalence about meeting another victim, or a sense of becoming overwhelmed are early alert signs. A support system of professionals who are not doing crisis counseling themselves will assist the operation and will prolong the staying power of the worker. Other measures also can be taken, including a change of schedule or retreat activities.

In summary, this chapter selects and describes a range of approaches and procedures for psychological intervention. These are analyzed within each of the developmental time phases of disaster assistance, and the authors suggest specific methodologies and techniques for use.

7

PHASE ONE:
THE FIRST FEW HOURS AND DAYS

This and the following two chapters present key categories of experiences and key concepts that evolve sequentially during the relief process. During each time phase, mental health practitioners face different environments and different psychological consequences and must therefore continually adapt their roles and use different skills. These chapters, then, describe mental health intervention during this relief process and give special attention to knowledge of the victim's setting or social conditions, mental health roles, and, lastly, interventive skills.

KNOWLEDGE: SOCIAL CONDITIONS

It is important for the mental health worker to have a complete understanding of the social conditions in the disaster area. In addition, the worker must view the disruption of these social conditions with the specifics of the disaster in mind. For effective organization of the proper mental health services, the worker must know:
- The type, kind, and intensity of the disaster;
- The length of the disaster and its warning period;
- The number of persons affected;
- The extent of property damage;
- The range and number of casualties; and
- The types of personal resources affected persons had at their disposal for combating disaster-related adversities.

The worker must also be aware of specific problems that will probably be encountered in assisting the postdisaster population. These problems will vary according to the type of disaster and the size of the community involved. For example, disasters such as earthquakes, tornados, and floods are usually marked by impacts that are short and sharp with little or no warning. Hurricanes and slow-rising floods are more likely to have an impact of longer duration with at least some warning period. If the disaster strikes a large urban community, a number of services and support lines of communication, such as telephones and transportation, will be disrupted and have a major impact on the situation.

During the earthquake in Managua, Nicaragua, in 1972, all the main hospitals in the city of 400,000 were destroyed and unfit to continue providing care for their patients and for the wounded in the disaster. The need to set up complete hospitalization systems using army tents donated by foreign countries demonstrated just one of the major reconstruction needs within the heart of a city.

In the urban setting, despite severe disruptions, assistance is generally readily available through the fairly large number of trained personnel in close proximity. Conversely, when the disaster strikes a rural area there are probably fewer services to be disrupted, but there are also proportionately fewer or sometimes no assistance services available.

These variations affect the types and the intensity of human problems that emerge and come to the attention of mental health professionals. The mobilization of the appropriate number and types of mental health personnel depends on the availability of data related to the needs of dispersed persons in the specific area. An important component of this appraisal is the assessment by the mental health planner of what has already been done by the people themselves and by the disaster assistance agencies involved. Information is required about what concrete services have already been provided and what disaster agencies, such as a Red Cross station, are on site. This assessment allows mental health workers to mobilize themselves rapidly toward forming a link with the Red Cross and other appropriate local, state, and federal agencies for joint participation in first-aid auxiliary assistance.

It is necessary to know the type and extent of physical damage—for example, what areas or buildings have been destroyed in the disaster area—in order to determine where the mental health teams can be placed and how they must be mobilized (cars, trucks, boats, helicopter) in the different geographical settings where the damage has occurred. As an example, the workers must know if the disaster victims as a group had to be relocated in temporary shelters or if there are some persons who stayed in their homes under duress. The types and placement of assistance given by public service agencies will make a difference as to how the mental health teams will be physically deployed so as to proceed jointly with overall planning. For example, do members of the team have to attend disaster planning meetings and provide assistance in different parts of a city, or is everyone congregated in a central command-post setting? All this information is preparatory to planning and allocating the mental health resources, which are finite and cannot proportionately meet the needs of all the disaster victims. Therefore careful resource allocation is called for in assigning aid where it is most needed, and it is precisely in these high-need areas that the professional mental health workers most require linkages with the work of the other recovery and assistance efforts.

CHARACTERISTICS OF THE SHELTER

When members of the mental health team enter a shelter, they must quickly appraise the grouping and social system arrangement to determine where the most help is needed and where the linking points with other teams should be developed for maximum organizational effectiveness. Usually the mental health team can offer the most assistance by linking with dispensers of services at the emergency health center. These include the Red Cross centers and/or the local, state, and federal service administrators who are coping with a multiplicity of human need.

It may be helpful to look at the activities of the team that participated in relief operations during the second day of the 1978 Massachusetts blizzard in one of the shelters. After members of the mental health group identified the leaders of the health system, the Red Cross, and several representatives of municipal government, a meeting was immediately called by one of the mental health professionals to discuss the organization of assistance programs and to develop a plan for collaboration. The concept of crisis counseling was introduced, and procedures for linking communication were suggested. This is the kind of action that was necessary for preliminary organization of services.

When a helpful and clear plan of action is presented amid an atmosphere of general confusion to a group of relatively inexperienced workers, it has a high possibility of being accepted and used. Information on the grouping and social system arrangement within the shelter, and on the process of collaboration and linkage with the National Guard and other forms of civil assistance, should be processed on a continuing and systematic basis, due to the rapid pace at which most events occur during the sequence of postdisaster activities. This allows for better understanding the various public agencies' missions and leads to coordination of their activities with those of the mental health teams. With this information, a mental health participation plan can be developed for preserving continuity through the various agency levels and changes in recovery planning operations.

This type of systematic approach is needed in trying to become organized amid the initial disorganization prevalent within the temporary shelter. The following account of a Red Cross supervisor's perceptions and personal reactions upon entering a shelter after the Massachusetts blizzard illustrates the sense of confusion:

During the last parts of this, Alan had arrived and was trying to get some sense of what all the shouting was about. I had just again cornered Mr. D. to try to find out what's what with the high school and can we use a few rooms for services when Dr. C. approaches us. Lose Mr. D. again because as Shelter Manager there are always at least three people waiting to talk with him.

Introductions made and some general information on what we're each doing passed, but my head is whirling with this political stuff and I don't need to know there's a public law that says mental health will be part of the relief process. It's obvious it's needed but I can't pull my own act together right now and that's needed, too.

Many of the people in and out of the rooms I've been in are wearing ill-fitting, wrinkled clothing. O.K. for now in this shelter, but it's soon going to really get to them if they can't start taking care of themselves, including getting into some of their own and/or new clothes.

So my attention wanders to where Mr. M. is now and who else might be around to open some of these numerous rooms and give me authority to use some for a few days.

My full attention swings back when I recognize that Dr. C. wasn't just trying to let us know they were around and would be involved somehow. She wanted to work with us and wanted to coordinate so the best services could be given to the victims. In my head that translated to one more thing that should be done immediately and I couldn't see resolution even close on what I was already involved with. But Alan was picking up quick on what this link could mean and was moving right along with it. Ended up exchanging phone numbers and it wasn't until we were driving back to Boston much later that I discovered Alan had pinned down something more definite for regrouping with Dr. C. to work out some details.

That came after finally getting together with the mayor and clarifying for him and the others there that a one-stop center is a ten-day to two-week phenomenon, not a six-month to one-year set-up, as they thought. That made the political hassles lessen significantly. The mayor had thought it was to be the city's responsibility to provide payment for a building, furniture, and all supportive systems necessary for this relief process to work. So that was a big load off his mind and a few more people started to get an inkling of what's going to happen. But I still don't have anything set up to start casework services tomorrow, and it's now a full five days after the storm.

Knowing the categories of recovery activities planning that need to be carried out is helpful in allocating the available time and energy to set up levels of operation. These categories are:

- Organizational planning of services with leaders of the other relief agencies;
- Consultation with and education for other professionals on mental health aspects that need to be added to the recovery services;
- Making others aware of the specialized functions of mental health professionals that can assist in aid to victims. In past disaster operations, these functions have generally been unavailable to agencies in developing recovery operations; therefore members of these

agencies have no experience or knowledge of how to conceptualize and make operational use of mental health professionals' skills; and

- Direct intervention and help for victims through a first-aid approach.

Efforts to keep up with the operational time frames of the other professionals require that continuous communication channels be kept open and that focus be maintained on tasks. This frame of reference should be kept in clear focus as procedures evolve.

Once it has been determined where the command-post or planning center of operations will be located and also where the mental health workers will be, the objectives of mental health professionals will become clearer to other disaster workers. This information will aid in evaluating how each group working in the setting can use the other's skills. It is also essential to the development of a good working rapport with the non-mental health workers and will help ensure the efficient mobilization of mental health staff resources to the disaster victims. For example, it is necessary not only to know how Red Cross workers function in shelters, but also to know how the specific individuals in this particular community have organized themselves.

Red Cross staff members are organized in most communities as a mixture of volunteers, with some staff members flown in from other regions specifically to organize the disaster assistance. Generally there are too few staff members able to grasp rapidly how to link with mental health professionals and how to use their skills. In several instances during the 1978 Massachusetts blizzard recovery operations, the Red Cross members were "surprised" at how helpful it was to add the experience of participating mental health professionals. They felt supported as they became aware of the potential assistance and the flexibility of approach offered by the mental health professionals, who could deal with the psychological problems presented by the victims. The same feeling applied to the National Guard, the civil defense, and the medical delivery systems. There are broad guidelines of how these groups are supposed to operate, but idiosyncratic and individualistic approaches by members of various agencies have to be noticed.

An example of the kind of organizational stalemate that can take place with a member of a collaborative agency occurred with a Red Cross supervisor in Massachusetts when one of the mental health professionals started designing the procedures that would guide their collaborative participation. As soon as a Red Cross worker identified a victim with emotional disturbances or psychological problems, he would call the mental health worker and ask for assistance. The stumbling block that appeared very soon in their negotiations was how the Red Cross worker would identify and introduce the mental health professional to the victim. The Red Cross worker acknowledged that he did not know what words to use and how to introduce the concept of psychiatric assistance for the victim's problems without feeling "guilty" about raising the suspicion that the victim needed a "shrink." A compromise was reached and the mental health professional was introduced as a crisis counselor participating in the federal program for disaster assistance.

CLUSTERING OF DISPLACED GROUPS

It is generally true that groups of varying sizes, composed of displaced family members or single individuals, cluster around the designated shelter areas provided by the authorities. It is important for mental health workers to identify these groups in terms of ethnic and socioeconomic characteristics. The immediate needs of these groups can be better satisfied if the workers have a clear understanding of the traditional customs and cultural backgrounds of those being helped. This will allow them to guide their helping approaches in a way that can be accepted and will fit the needs of the victims, for it is the special characteristics of the groups that affect behavior patterns during the initial crisis period.

The concept of cultural sensitivity can be exemplified by this case history of one victim in a shelter:

A fifty-year-old Italian barber was sitting in a rather dejected fashion on the cot that had been assigned to him. The mental health worker approached him and asked him how things were. He started telling the story about his home that had been inundated by a storm's waves and how they had destroyed most of his basement, where he had a freezer that had just recently been fully stocked. He had spent hundreds of dollars to get the food, especially meat, for his family. He went on to say that he had been able to handle most of the trouble, even though he had the harrowing experience of having to wait for a boat to pick him up while he and his family sat and watched the water come in and recede in the basement. What had finally produced an unbearable stress and shock feeling was passing by his barber shop as he was being rescued in a boat. He saw that it had been vandalized and could not accept this. He broke down sobbing and crying as he expressed his dismay that there could be people who would do this to him. He had tried to keep a "stiff upper lip, as a man should," but lost control at the sight of the pilfered shop.

ROLE CONFIGURATION

Presented here is a detailed outline of the role of mental health workers as they should function during the first forty-eight hours after a a disaster has occurred. The specific functions of the mental health worker during this postdisaster stage are discussed both as part of the procedures of psychological assistance and as part of more concrete postdisaster services, such as obtaining resources to benefit the victims in collaboration with other agencies (e.g., the Red Cross or various local, state, and federal relief programs).

The role of the mental health professional who works with staff from other agencies and with public officials involved in directing disaster operations is still ambiguous but also an integral part of the relief effort. The evolution of these alternate roles, as practiced within new community crisis settings, has an impact on traditionally developed mental health clinical roles. Expectations of mental health professionals, both by themselves and others, present some difficulties and problems in the level of comfort experienced by workers in disaster assistance functions. For example, at one point during the Massachusetts blizzard relief aid, Red Cross staff shared their observations of how they perceived mental health workers. They felt that the mental health workers were not clear in their approaches and showed confused behavior. Although there was no question about their sincere interest in servicing the victims and in being helpful, the professionals appeared ill at ease, unsure of what to do next, and not very clear about the modality of participatory activities in the shelter.

Traditional concepts of mental health workers as being clearly aware of their own functions and duties within the clinical framework and also cognizant of expected behavior (as perceived by their colleagues) are altered in a postdisaster assistance setting. It appears that traditional behavior must be adequately adapted to fit the different sets of needs and timely demands for action operating during a disaster. These needs include the ability of the mental health worker who has access to only minimal data to work rapidly and flexibly in collaboration with other disaster aid professionals. In working with the Red Cross, volunteers, and civil defense workers, problems such as trust, communication style, and familiarity of mutual tasks emerge, and collaborative solutions may not yet be clearly identified and developed. There are issues of tradition, problems of working together related to professional differences in cultural and value systems, and conflicting ideologies on how to help disaster victims. Problems arise from different role expectations, status, and behavior; these are coupled with differing expectations within the various mental health disciplines—M.D.'s, social workers, nurses, and others—that make up the team.

The following example illustrates the problems of role definition and expectations ("What am I supposed to do, and what is everyone else doing or supposed to be doing?"). The account is a Red Cross supervisor's perception upon first entering a temporary shelter:

The following two days we did start doing the immediate assistance at the high school. I believe it was the first of the two days that a young man showed up and identified himself as a psychiatrist. He wasn't sure what he was supposed to be doing, nor were we. Even though the caseload was relatively small that day (about forty-five, I believe), it was our first day and we were (1) feeling out what each of our co-workers was capable of doing; (2) trying to establish the most efficient physical set-up to give the greatest privacy possible for caseload processing; (3) trying to find out from the shelter manager what had happened up to that point and get a feel of who was who in the community and how they might help or hinder our relief process; (4) dealing with the general confusion and anxiety produced by the state coming in, taking people out of the shelter, and placing them in hotels (how were we to find them later if they didn't seek us out?).

John spent some time with the psychiatrist but was involved in solving some crisis or another, so I spent some time describing what the Red Cross does in disaster relief, relating some of the problems that people were going to have, and speculating about how our workers would link people to him. As there were no obvious problems right then, I believe I suggested he spend time in the waiting room and if he noticed anyone who was particularly anxious or depressed, he could talk with them. I think I did see him in the waiting room once after that, but when we had a person who could obviously use his help, he was gone. (I vaguely remember his coming to me and saying he had a case he had to work on at his clinic and was leaving.) This was disappointing, because it was later in the afternoon and most of us were frazzled, too.

I believe what happened the first several days is that early in the day when we were fresh (as were the disaster victims), we were inclined to handle situations, including victims' emotional problems, as part of our normal caseload process. We had patience and were mentally alert, so could provide emotional support along with the material relief process. If that happened, the people who were there to provide mental health services would think they weren't needed, lose interest, and tend to get back to their regular jobs, where they knew they were needed. That means they were gone by the time our energy was depleted and we could no longer handle clients' stress on top of our own.

As the process went on a few more days and we had a clearer picture of the delineation between our straight material assistance procedure and the crisis intervention procedure, we were more able to turn over problem situations, even when we were able to intervene ourselves.

The role of the mental health worker cannot be developed merely through interconnections with other disaster agency members who help give that role status and legitimacy. True, these interconnections help develop and guide the objectives of mental health intervention. However, constant awareness of their roles by the mental health workers themselves will help them understand their functions; this in turn allows them to perform their duties effectively.

This new role definition needs to be immediately, energetically, and systematically developed before it can be acknowledged and accepted both by other mental health professionals and by workers from disaster assistance agencies. As groups develop and tend to link agency members, continued role clarification has to be shared. This is accomplished by making agreements, negotiations, and verbal contracts to provide answers consistently for questions raised by the situations that emerge when people are trying to solve problems. Asking "What do I do now? How can I be of assistance?" while at the same time asking "What can *you* do? How can *you* be of assistance to the victim?" is a means of providing for a consistent mode of response as a myriad of situations is presented.

This method of task division among different groups to facilitate and organize relief assistance is evident in the following approach, which shows how responsibilities were divided and assigned among a group of citizens and professionals from Managua, and another group of professionals from the United States, who were all working together after the 1972 Nicaraguan earthquake. A large percentage of citizens were deployed to temporary housing in the camp "America" (a row of wooden houses built by the Agency for International Development), where outreach workers would go from door to door looking for citizens with problems or difficulties. When they identified someone who, in their estimation, needed help, they would refer him to a special team housed in one of the small, temporary wooden homes in the camp where all the citizens had been relocated. Here psychologists from the American team, assisted by a group of students from the Managua University, obtained histories and did mental status exams. When a serious case showing the symptoms of acute crisis needed further psychological or psychiatric intervention, the person would be referred to a backup psychiatric team that operated in one of the existing outpatient sites in the city. This group of professionals, paraprofessionals, and volunteers would meet at the end of the day and rapidly exchange information or receive instructions on how to assist victims; in this way everyone's skills and interests were enhanced as much as possible.

Because of the continuous shifting due to constant relocation procedures, standard behavioral guidelines should be developed and implemented to facilitate informed and efficient problem solving among all the organized disaster relief professionals, who continue to shift roles as time goes by. Harmonious agreements and minimal conflict must be achieved so that the helping groups are ready to work and have enough energy to support and guide the painfully disorganized life and world of the victims.

SKILLS

After assessing the social situation surrounding the postdisaster behavior of victims, it is time to address methods of intervention. Decisions must be made on how mental health workers should intervene through a first-aid auxiliary approach, and what procedures should be instituted to help the victims cope by gaining a sense of control over their shifting, unfamiliar, and stressful environment. First, it is necessary for the mental health worker to practice the basic techniques for developing and establishing a relationship with a person who is showing distressed behavior. This technique is known to practitioners dealing with individuals in crisis. Second, it is necessary for mental health workers to familiarize themselves with expected individual reactions to the experience of surviving a disaster. The following dialogue between a mental health counselor and a victim shows the emotional reaction to a disaster:

> *Mental health counselor:* I'm interested in how you are feeling. What have your experiences been like?"
>
> *Victim:* "Well, it was very depressing. I was trying to figure out what I could do, and yet I couldn't seem to get any answers of what I was going to do. I more or less got to the point where we were going to have to play it by ear and let people take over. I knew it was going to take an awful lot of time to straighten out. Don't matter who help you, you couldn't replace, you couldn't put things back in place the way they were. It was gone. Whatever was there was gone—which turned out to be so true. With all the help they gave you, which you were very grateful for, it still didn't replace, it still didn't put things back the way they were. The people didn't even know what the damage was that they had suffered. They were there in their shelter, they had left everying, and they didn't know what was going to be there when they got back. Things were still up in the air so far as that goes."

This victim is expressing her sense of loss and trying to explain to herself what has happened.

The repertoire of mental health intervention skills and the objectives of intervention during the first phase of the postdisaster experience can be conceptualized procedurally in terms of a "first-aid" effort. This psychological assistance is in the form of face-to-face intervention assistance to victims. This is their first step in reorienting and adapting themselves to their new transitory reality, the first step in beginning to resolve their crisis. The disaster victims need help with reality testing in order to assess what has happened, what is happening, and what will happen. Extreme care should be taken not to interfere with defense mechanisms used by victims to remain in control. An example of handling of emotions by denial mechanisms is shown in the dialogue with a rescued victim:

> *Question:* "How did you feel about the fact that the evacuation people were taking so long to get to you? Or did you just figure, 'what can I do?'"

Answer: "Well, I was kinda angry, but I had to put myself in their shoes, too. How much can they do? How many men are there? How much equipment do they have? See, you have to have that equipment ready—that's the big thing right there; You have to have the equipment. You could need 300 men and they only have like 20. If you only have one boat, what good are they?"

The crisis counselor agreed with the reality. He supported the sensitivity and adaptation to this first unreal traumatic experience and did not try to stimulate the contained and defended rage. For the immediate situation of the victim, being in control is the main objective of counseling.

A mental health worker should couple the techniques used to aid and support a victim reacting to the stress produced directly from the disaster with techniques appropriate to the emotional reactions and sensations characteristic of one who is a member of a displaced group in a public shelter. In addition, the relationships between counselors and victims must be nurtured continuously. Workers must express empathy without acting out either a sense of omnipotence or a rescue fantasy. They must quickly appraise mental status (cognitive and defensive functions; level of anxiety, depression, fear, or anger), and relate appropriately to help victims. They should combine respectful expressions of support with the utmost efficiency of time use—an important technique for mental health workers to acquire during this stage. A balance must be struck between expressing empathy and reinforcing and rewarding "the victim role." The worker must also become aware of the healthier parts of the victim's personality and mobilize them to enhance the ability to "hold on" for the time being. One useful technique is to promise (if feasible) to see the person for another short period during that same day or the next.

A middle-age widow was asking for assistance from the shelter Red Cross worker, incessantly firing one question after another. Were they going to be relocated? Were they going to get enough help? Could she get money to fix her home? When could she return to her house to find one of her pets? The counselor was called and proceeded to identify a high level of anxiety in an angry, compulsive personality. After allowing the victim to share her troubles and fears about living in such close proximity to others, the counselor obtained data about future moves and promised the next day she would inform her of the schedule. They established a ten-minute meeting every morning, and the victim became an active participant in the group shelter. Her anxiety diminished, and she assisted one of the nurses with scheduling chores for other victims.

While the mental health workers are developing and shifting through the roles of planner, consultant, collaborator, and counselor, they must continuously be aware of their own limitations of strength, the contagiousness of the victim's fear and anger, and their own susceptibility to it. They also must guard against strong, seductive, and omnipotent fantasies of rescuing the victims. The experience is intensely personal and heart wrenching. There will be emotional upheavals in dealing with disaster victims, and rescue workers who are not sure about their own coping resources and who overtax their coping abilities will have trouble during the first few days after the disaster in keeping a balanced awareness of reality.

In summary, for the first two to three days mental health workers base aid procedures upon the diagnosis of the crisis behavior shown by the victims. They will sort out priorities for intervention, such as helping with a victim's sense of orientation, reinforcing reality testing, developing support and trust, and ascertaining a victim's need for resources available through other agencies. In addition to the development of support systems around victims, there is also the development of a de facto system within the victim group in the temporary shelters. The great array of resources available must be supported and organized to meet the specific needs of the victims. Many of these needs are concrete, but some are psychological. The mental health worker, ascertaining this, can then mobilize appropriate psychological help by observing the way other agencies or groups approach the victim, and by consultation in order to bring appropriate resource allocation to them. This requires a special type of technique that allows mental health workers to elicit directly and personally from the victims, in their own communication style, what they perceive as immediate needs; to interpret this content; and then to collaborate with other agencies and mobilize their resources so that the victims feel assisted, less helpless, less hopeless, and less destitute. To lessen the stress is the primary objective of this phase.

8

PHASE TWO:
THE FIRST FEW WEEKS

KNOWLEDGE

The development of a temporary infrastructure composed of human structures forming collaborative links between the mental health worker and the other agencies sets the stage for program development in the second phase of a disaster. Further objectives and activities of mental health workers are identified, and these progress as the workers join the larger systems of assistance operations that begin to grow and acquire clearer patterns and structures within days after the disaster. It is necessary to realize that emergency assistance units like the Red Cross have their own objectives, approaches, and procedures, and that their local operations are components of a much larger national system—of which they are "out-stations" in the specific disaster setting.

Procedures similar to those used in the shelters must be developed to guide mental health professionals in joint problem solving with government representatives or other disaster agency members, who represent extensions of much larger and more complex organizations. There will be variations on how administrative links with the mental health teams are formalized, and how various individuals accept the progressive introduction of mental health concepts and approaches into their own systems.

An example of the difficulty in establishing communication links in the middle of a disaster assistance intervention emerged in Massachusetts in 1978, when much of the personal data Red Cross workers got from distraught victims were not available to mental health workers because of confidentiality requirements. The Red Cross staff had not negotiated prior permission to share names and descriptions of personal episodes with mental health workers, who were interested in follow-through and subsequent visits to victims' homes to offer crisis counseling on a longer term basis than in the one-stop centers, which would close after several weeks. Because of regional or national regulations, it was impossible to share the data.

In this situation, activities and meetings were set up with both district and regional Red Cross staff to continue developing a collaborative, professional relationship and to plan for the possibility of exchanging case information in the future. These activities further clarified the complexities of legitimization and sanction within collaborative service models. This procedure can vary, depending on whether the mental health effort is originating from a neighborhood satellite clinic, from a person who is the sole representative of mental health efforts, from workers representing mental health centers or clinics, or from official representatives of central and area departments of mental health.

For the mental health workers, an understanding of the different approaches tied to sanction, power, and the number of mental health resources (staff, time, etc.) is important in forming a workable plan. This is particularly crucial, considering that mental health systems are still in the early stages of developing roles and functions and of receiving and accepting postdisaster responsibility. Major efforts to participate, to develop procedures, and to establish relationships with disaster agencies will have to be initiated and pushed forward by the mental health governmental systems, both formally and informally, in order to achieve a status of professional usefulness in disaster assistance. Important variables for success appear to be based on the premise that official mental health personnel must be rapid in their decision making; must be efficient, with minimal wasting of other agency workers' time; and must independently accept tasks with a minimal reliance on guidance or support from the other representatives, who are themselves overwhelmed by their own tasks. Victim demands for all kinds of assistance and a general lack of familiarity with most helpers form the backdrop for those variables. Participating mental health teams must deal with those variables as they continue to offer assistance in the first few postdisaster weeks.

The following case highlights some of these issues:

Mental health professionals working with a Red Cross team in a federal center set up in a devastated town had established a method by which, when the Red Cross workers saw an individual who manifested psychological distress, they would invite the mental health professionals to participate with them in their interview. The Red Cross workers called for help in the case of a 40-year-old, white, single woman who was confused, upset, and angry at the fact that she had been relocated from a high school shelter to a single house with a family. There she was renting a room but had no access to the amenities of the house, including a television. She had lost the apartment she was renting because the house was damaged and her car was flooded. She was an assistant bookkeeper, but was so distressed that she had been unable to go back to work. She was asking assistance from the Red Cross in relocating to a motel and getting a loan to repair her car.

Because of her psychological distress, this woman was unable to articulate her needs; thus the mental health professional was asked to assist the Red Cross worker in sorting out those needs. After getting some of the required background data, the rest of the interview was devoted mainly to the woman's ventilation of her anger and her sense of loss of a familiar setting, symbolized by her inability to use the television at her convenience and leisure in the rented room. As her rage diminished and she felt supported, she became more organized in her thinking and clearer in sorting out what she wanted. It was evident that it would be almost impossible to reroute her to group housing in a motel, but that she would have to mobilize herself from the rented room to an apartment. When this task was presented, she again regressed to her infantile dependent position, saying she didn't know how to find an apartment, that she had no car and wanted someone to drive her. This again precipitated another circular pattern of asking, denying needs, begging for help, and refusing to participate in a collaborative manner to think about how one goes about getting an apartment. With further support of her anger and despair, she began to talk concretely about how, by looking through the newspaper and possibly getting a friend to drive her, she might find a suitable place. The victim and the mental health worker then talked with the staff of several agencies involved in providing the appropriate resources.

This case shows the complexity of mental health intervention, which must help mobilize the healthy, coping resources of traumatized victims so they can function in the large bureaucracy set up to assist hundreds of people at the same time. Disaster victims often feel frustrated by trying to deal with all the required paper work and may become annoyed with standing in long lines waiting their turn to be allocated resources that fit their specific needs. The mental health professional will have to reach out actively to other agencies and support systems to develop an "action plan" that moves the victims further along in the quest of re-aligning their life settings.

ROLE

The mental health worker must observe and learn how the local, state, and federal resource agents such as the Red Cross, health department, and civil defense are distributing and organizing their personnel. This understanding must be gained within new physical settings established to process help to victims. At this time the linkages established by the mental health team should continue to enhance the collaboration and systematic service coordination started during these first weeks. New group dynamics between the care-giving personnel emerge, and some agency conflict or personal difficulties become clearer. Also needed at this time is current knowledge of any new regulations from higher authorities within the helping systems or agencies: these will have an impact on the delivery of resources at the neighborhood level. This knowledge is important for mental health workers so they can mobilize and use auxiliary resources for the benefit of victims.

In mental health disaster assistance it is not productive to use only psychological techniques or to see this procedure as one to be practiced independently of all the other events occurring in and surrounding the living space of the victim. All available assistance resources must be understood and mobilized, incorporating psychological interaction with concrete aid available from the Red Cross and other disaster relief agencies. Victims expect more than just personal interaction. They need shelter, food, money, clothes, and transportation, and all this aid must be integrated.

Major needs of life situations, as well as the victims' expectations of assistance on a concrete level, would make psychological interactions by themselves meaningless to the victim. *The knowledge of how and where to obtain concrete resources, coupled with the appropriate psychological way to help and to offer these resources to the victim as part of the total assistance effort, defines and differentiates psychological disaster assistance from traditional mental health assistance in clinics and hospitals.*

Differentiating degrees of disaster efforts within federal or local assistance networks is also necessary. Whether the victim has suffered a major or minimal loss is the question raised over and over again by all workers. There seems to be a rule of thumb among experienced agency staff that people who have suffered total loss will need more of everything in the first stages of relief operations. By asking this question they begin to sort out the two categories. The following excerpts from a taped conversation between a disaster victim and a mental health worker clearly illustrates the victim's feelings of loss, confusion, and helplessness when confronted with trying to arrange for assistance within the one-stop center for help in reordering her world:

And then one day they opened the place at the church—was it Tuesday? We went down to the place, but the way they treated us—like we didn't know how to do things. Wait in line. Get numbers. Not even offering you a cup of coffee—that was awful. Then you were all confused. You didn't know where to go first. They gave you a number: you are going to go to this one, you are going to go to that one . . . so many places to go and things to do. . . .

I still did not want to come back to the house. Did you know that? You couldn't get me to come near this house for six weeks. Every time I would come here, I would sit in the car but I wouldn't come in this house. I just didn't want to come back here because this has been the second time we've had a storm. The third time, it is going to take my life.

They told me to go to the housing desk. I figured they would find me temporary housing. . . . They said go to HUD—that's the housing agency. I didn't know it had something to do with a big agency; as far as I knew it was just for housing. They were going to help me out and find me a house. It took me twenty years to build up my home like this and it took a half hour to destroy it. I can't even cry anymore. I don't have any tears left. And they said they were going to help us with the house. Then they kept asking us, do we want to rent a house? I can't remember; I tell you the truth I can't remember.

Next thing I remember is that my little girl was very sick. I thought I could not handle anything more. At this point we didn't have much strength left; it really affected us mentally. I look at my poor kid and she won't even go near the house. She's scared too. I'm scared. Where are we going to go? We haven't got a dime. All our money is in the house.

So we start coming back here. What were they going to do? Everytime you looked across the floor somebody had tears on them. It was like we were all in a dream. Like my friend across sitting on her cot—her mother is 90 years old, and the poor old soul couldn't stay where she was. She got very sick. . . . She had to go over to her son's house, and she was crying. The poor woman didn't know what she was going to do. Her home was all flooded.

We were all in the same boat in the high school, sitting there feeling dejected, not knowing what was going to happen to us. If you ask anybody else, no one knew anything. It was awful. Like you were on people's mercy. We didn't know where we were going to go and we didn't care. All you cared about was not to go back in the house with all the water. We didn't know anything. We didn't know where we were going until the last Saturday night, when we made out some forms and they first said they were going to take us to the Ramada Inn. Then they won't take us, and we have to go to another motel. Stayed there one night, went to the Howard Johnson. We didn't know that till the last minute; nobody explained anything to us. You go up and ask anything and they say, "We don't know anything about it." I guess perhaps they didn't know. . . . You know what I mean?

The role of the mental health worker continues to be defined in terms of the various evolving expectations, activities, and behavior practiced in the changing housing arrangements and the one-stop center as the days go by. The role develops further as the workers become aware of the type of assistance they can provide in coordination with and as a supplement to other aid. The professional also interacts with the planning groups of the disaster program and supports the expectation of adding mental health components to the design and delivery of programs. In the past, these plans evolved without incorporating mental health input. Now mental health objectives can emerge as part of the overall plans and assisting procedures to be organized and deployed. Other agencies begin to expect the mental health professional to be a diagnostician in problems of behavioral and emotional expressions; they are expected to treat and prescribe for individuals with problems, including diagnosis of drugs and alcohol abuse. They also view the mental health worker as consultant, convener, and collaborator. The psychiatrist is expected to double as a physician because of his ability to diagnose and prescribe medications. Mental health professionals will increasingly be seen as members of the disaster assistance team as they are given trust and responsibility, as they participate in difficult logistic resource allocations in programs, and as they attend problem-solving meetings at all levels of agency planning.

Collaborative behavior in disaster assistance can be viewed as the mental health professional actively helping an agency worker and taking part of the responsibility for dealing with individual or group problems. This kind of behavior enables mental health professionals not only to discuss and advise, but to participate in implementing a plan for the victim. They share the responsibility of resolving problem situations, as they and the agency workers act together in ways appropriate to their respective professional training and roles. Mental health professionals may visit families with the agency workers to get reports of damage and loss. They may be part of a group discussion composed of two or three agency representatives and a victim. They may visit families alone and then go to the agency setting to discuss and share recommendations. In collaborative situations, both mental health and agency workers continually have direct contact with victims and families, and both contribute to the actual support program.

Coordination includes those efforts that mental health professionals pursue when they endeavor to link together individuals or agencies who participate in the resource allocation and support program of a given victim. There is a need to schedule time for this to happen. Opportunities for group and decision meetings, and opportunities for discussion among individual helpers on the feasibility of sharing responsibility, have to occur if collaborative efforts are to be part of postdisaster intervention. There is a danger that, due to the intensity and enormity of most recovery efforts, such efforts may become fragmented and poorly aligned to meet the multiple needs of the victim. Thus a discontinuous network of services becomes established. A mental health professional who is sensitive to systems design can prevent some of the frustrating experiences in store for victims who get lost in the bureaucratic maze of assistance efforts, a maze where all the workers are trying to do their best within logistic systems that are difficult to control.

To develop and incorporate this role internally, mental health professionals must add two new important value objectives to their repertoire of interventive work skills. The first value objective involves developing an ability to assist, in a collegiate-therapeutic approach, members of other agencies who are providing concrete relief resources to victims. The mental health worker must first help the victims articulate their immediate needs. Because the victims are understandably distraught, they are often unable to express their needs adequately and thus may not receive sufficient assistance from an agency worker. The following account exemplifies a double level of intervention where the Red Cross worker, along with a mental health professional, was able to observe an intervention and to follow through in a supportive manner:

The Red Cross worker saw a woman who appeared upset and depressed and asked a mental health worker to assist her. The woman, a 35-year-old married, white citizen of a town that had been destroyed by a storm, related that her husband had been hospitalized with severe chest pains the day after the disaster. Her daughter had to go live with another neighbor because there had not been temporary housing for the whole family, and a son was living with a young friend and two older men in an apartment. The woman had finally been given an apartment to move to in a nearby town and had accepted it. When she asked her son to move in with her, he refused and became belligerent and hostile. It was evident the relationships in the family had been ambivalent even before the disaster, but because of events subsequent to the disaster family ties had broken.

The mental health worker supported and helped the woman ventilate and express her pain, encouraging her to cry and to share the story. The worker then called the supervisor of schools, who was in the shelter, to help the mother put together a plan of action. That plan would use the expertise of the guidance counselor of the school her son was attending to explore the problems further. The woman was able to control herself, her crying eventually diminished, her facial expression began to show more liveliness, and there were signs of hope when she accepted, in writing, the name and telephone number of the crisis counselor with whom she was going to continue working. She then turned to the Red Cross worker and was able to articulate clearly a list of things she needed for relocation.

The second value objective involves the mental health worker learning how to offer assistance rapidly, effectively, and efficiently, according to the psychological and physiological reactions experienced by the victim, and then to collaborate with the other agents to serve the victim on both a psychological and physical basis. The rapid method of intervention could be exemplified by this case:

A 40-year-old white woman was despondent and upset while her husband was going through an episode of alcohol withdrawal symptoms. He refused to be driven to a detoxification center, and his wife was too upset to convince him or exert any influence on modifying his position. While he was being seen by the medical doctor, a mental health professional worked with her and was able to elicit a story of long suffering and difficulties in marital relations before the disaster. There had been several times when they were going to separate and then got back together, with the husband always promising that he would stop drinking. It was evident that the relationship was characterized by a masochistic bonding, the wife passively allowing the relationship to deteriorate until she couldn't stand it and then separating as the only way of exerting any influence on her husband's drinking. It was also evident that the wife was not able to stay by herself in the shelter while the husband would be driven to the hospital, unless the mental health workers would promise to get them back together and obtain a ride for her so that she could see him the next day. Finally she agreed and made a decision to follow the advice of the physician which, once put into execution, produced a dramatic change in her, diminishing her symptoms of despondency and crisis tension.

The status of the mental health professional begins to emerge as all these roles become clarified and appreciated by both the victims and the other disaster workers.

SKILLS

The mental health intervention skills used during the first days after the disaster should continue to grow and proceed along set guidelines, beginning with the triage approach discussed before and adding other types of short therapeutic interventions. Objectives should be set for rapidly ascertaining personality structure, mental status, needs, and sources of trouble as a victim proceeds through life events and settles into assigned new housing. Adding to the former postdisaster stresses are the many new problems that arise as groups of people are processed through group schedules and organized procedures set up to meet the logistic demands of assigning housing, resources, food vouchers, etc. What victims really need during this stage is to share actively in some of this planning and to become interrelated with the authority system in such a way that their actions become meaningful to them. Response to the loss of concrete things, accustomed life styles, and daily routines begins to emerge as victims enter the formal bureaucratic system of postdisaster assistance. This further emphasizes the difficulties the victims will face in dealing with their new lives, which continue to change almost daily. Loss of familiar space produces a "schema" confusion that interferes with ritualistic, customary modes of daily behavior; this in turn disrupts planning and anticipatory actions.

Each of the mental health skills necessary for helping victims is influenced by the issue of "turf." Lack of familiarity with the setting and new patterns of relationships in work produce stress and uncertainty for the mental health worker. Obviously, one's professional behavior in such unfamiliar settings must reflect and adapt to the new reality. The resulting new approaches will emphasize collaboration with other relief agencies in giving psychological assistance to victims.

The following is an example. After a team of mental health professionals got funding for a six-month disaster aid program, it was necessary to develop linkages to the other disaster agencies and local groups that were supporting citizens through the months of reconstructing their homes and lives. A referral system to the project workers was formed, and meetings began regularly. This team continued to work with the ongoing disaster assistance agencies, so that all the workers involved would know what the service program would look like, what the victims were asking for, and what crisis counseling could offer. The information was shared as assistance activities were phased out in the one-stop center.

For emergency relief operations within the dispersed temporary housing, workers must continue to collaborate with Red Cross volunteers, medical personnel, and any other persons who directly participate with the victims, wherever they may be lodged within the living arrangements. When victims are in need of rapid assistance, the logistics of communication can be one of the most difficult problems, and technology is crucial.

The mental health workers' activities involve diagnosing a situation socially, emotionally, and physiologically, while determining what methods and procedures to use in helping the victims return to a functional, self-integrated level of behavior within temporary housing conditions or their own damaged abodes. Short-term procedures that should be instituted include:

- Extending and reinforcing the victims' support systems (family or agency);
- Linking the victims to recovery assistance;
- Convening resources around the victims;
- Psychotherapeutic procedures; and
- Using mild sedation or obtaining medication for posthospitalized, mentally diagnosed patients.

It is important to remember that the objectives of working in temporary housing are always short term. These shelters are not the places to begin crisis or short-term therapy because changes are always imminent. It can only be a brief operation, and a crisis counseling center that is functioning in an artificial and temporary environment sets up procedures knowing that the victim has to be supported, aided to express emotions, and guided until further planning for long-term relocation begins. During this period the knowledge of where each of the victims will be living afterwards must be obtained; longer term psychological objectives can then be ascertained and provided.

9

PHASE THREE:
THE FIRST FEW MONTHS

KNOWLEDGE: THE SOCIAL SETTING OF THE VICTIM

The high levels of anger and frustration experienced by victims during the first few months after a disaster are heightened by various psychodynamic reactions to the necessary shifts in living locations. Other factors contributing to the frustration include an increasing awareness of what has been lost, difficulty in understanding how to get fiscal and economic relief, physical fatigue, emotional stress, and continuous change in the degree of personal comfort. Generally, the shelters for large groups are closed within a short period of time. Victims are then relocated and housed in temporary settings such as trailers, wooden houses (as in Managua), hotels, and motels. Some move in with relatives or friends, while others return to damaged housing and begin to patch it up.

The shifting world of the victims in the postdisaster months presents new sets of stresses in addition to those generated by the initial crisis. The physical settings offered to the victims by agencies, relatives, or friends present different logistics and resource-development problems for mental health professionals, who must now go out and locate the dispersed victims. One advantage is that they find the victims developing new environments that provide a greater degree of personal comfort and privacy and some freedom to organize their lives according to their own desires and styles. Smaller, more private physical surroundings in which to meet and talk present different opportunities for interaction between the mental health worker and the victim. Because the situation is more centrally focused on individual family members, the techniques and skills necessary to intervene begin to approximate the traditional and known techniques of mental health professionals.

While these temporary arrangements are progressing, a parallel major mental health activity is ending with the closing of the one-stop centers.

Just as the mental health workers are developing an understanding of how this setting functions, of the objectives and activities of other agency representatives within that setting, and of the type of personnel assigned by the government, the center is closed. The specific agency documentation necessary to obtain further assistance or resources, the official regulations, the conditions and constraints for mental health workers—all continue to change. The mental health worker who may have just begun to develop an organization of services must also change and move on. A dispersed resources allocation model must be created, although the group of agencies that must remain in close contact may vary from community to community.

It is essential for the leader of the mental health team to ascertain all these new changes in time to make plans relevant to the other disaster agencies' patterns of change. He or she must understand how the new arrangements work, and develop relationships with the new, multilevel leaders of local, state, and federal agencies, as well as special private agencies within the community.

The longer reconstructive efforts and mental health planning activities should determine where continued collaboration will occur. This in turn will set the stage for linking agencies to participate in further collaborations and for determining how resources around victims will be systematically organized for mental health interventions in the following months.

The developmental and evolutionary process started during the first few hours of the disaster among the groups assisting victims enters a new stage with new problems, including those of communication. A complex of work boundaries, agency power structure conflicts, agency objectives modification, and differing levels of skills and sophistication of professionals and lay workers all emerge and add to the many difficulties in exchanging accurate information. There is a need to review verbal contracts made among workers and to remind the appropriate personnel of these agreements during these sequential shifts of location. This becomes especially necessary because of busy phone signals and distorted messages conveyed by victims, and because of all the new helpers now appearing on the scene, such as real estate appraisers, plumbers, carpenters, and so forth.

The impact and characteristics of the disaster continue to change as the intensity, disorganization, and level of confusion begin to diminish in general among the care givers and the victims. The developmental stages of adaptation to reality, crisis resolution, and the psychological environment of the victim shift in a parallel fashion. Victims begin to present individual, specific characteristics associated with different levels of adaptation that fluctuate over time. Those victims who will eventually be more vulnerable to mild or moderate psychological or physiological decompensation will begin to show signs of psychophysiologic stress as a reconstitution of the crisis. They will begin to seek and accept aid in larger numbers in the counseling centers. As an example, the following case illustrates how one victim was helped by the concerted efforts of both the mental health worker and the more traditional dispensers of concrete aid:

A widow, 56 years old, had always lived in the beach area of a town hit by a hurricane. The woman asked for counseling assistance through some friends. She complained of weakness, had lost fifteen pounds, and found herself very nervous. She looked agitated and cried very easily. She had lost her husband five years previously and lived alone. The victim also talked constantly and spontaneously and was preoccupied by the delay in obtaining the funds promised by the federal assistance agency and by not being able to get reimbursement for the workers she wanted to hire to fix her home. She wanted her own workers instead of having them sent by the agency. The agency insisted that they would send workers, but she did not trust them, did not wait, and hired her own people. Now she owed them money and had received a bill for the work done independent of "government guidelines." She still needed a substantial amount of repair work and felt that what the workers did as a part of minimal repairs was not enough. Her stress symptoms seemed related to her dissatisfaction with the fact that official agents did not seem to respond to her letters and phone calls. She also received the wrong set of forms when she asked for a grant and a loan and had been denied fiscal assistance for the furniture she lost because the loss was not well documented.

The woman complained that she had great difficulties in daily functioning and in dealing with the agencies "because I don't have a man." It was clear that, although there were several real disaster-based problems, her dependency needs flooded and overwhelmed her. She was still mourning and dealing with only partially resolved bereavement feelings. Her defense mechanisms, weakened by the disaster stress and aftermath events, were not able to contain her conflicts within a rigid and obsessive personality structure that did not allow her to deal with rage and anger.

The victim felt that she did not know how to deal with a "masculine" world. The mental health worker was able to guide her through all the intricacies of dealing with the agencies and receiving more appropriate support. She also helped the woman get in touch with a good support system that she had not utilized: a large family nearby and many good friends. In addition, the counselor helped her remember the times when she and her husband were able to handle some difficulties, and this rekindled her awareness of personal skills.

After six or seven visits, the victim appeared much better. But shortly after that she called again, and when visited she appeared agitated and exhausted, showing signs of speech pressures and insomnia. Her problem was that "I have not paid my bills and people are expecting their money which I don't have." It appears that the check to pay some of the bills got lost and some of the payments were delayed. The worker contacted the appropriate agent, began to straighten it out, and told the woman to call back in two days if she had not heard anything. She called a day or two later saying "I couldn't wait any longer, so I walked to the agency and was able to straighten out the communication mishap." After that she was able to get a handle on her emotions and sustain the anxiety of waiting.

One more episode occurred when there was a mix-up about an unpaid bill and the woman walked to town with her sister to talk rather angrily with an individual at the agency. Afterwards she called the worker and felt extremely guilty about "blasting him" and was afraid that she had antagonized him and would not receive her money. When she did receive the money a week later she felt better, appeared to regain control over her behavior, related comfortably with the worker, and reported that all her symptoms had disappeared. This women needed to see her "concrete" world return to a semblance of her previous one. This happened when she paid all her bills.

ROLE OF THE MENTAL HEALTH WORKER

The role of the mental health worker undergoes another major shift when the activities become divided along two levels between individuals, temporary, family-focused shelters and the centralized offices of agencies for resource distribution and mental health assistance. Role expectations, developed in the temporary shelters, about what the mental health assistance will encompass reappear at this time. The role of the mental health worker may suffer a dislocation and become vague or confusing to members of other agencies who, for the most part, have returned to their central offices. The victims suffer a similar confusion and may wonder just what the mental health workers can do for them at this stage of the reconstruction of their homes and lives.

For example, if a victim is having difficulty in obtaining money or other resources to repair a damaged house, s/he may see little or no use in "merely talking with the mental health worker" even though s/he may be suffering from insomnia, intense discomfort with aggressive feelings, or crying spells. It is again necessary for the mental health worker to develop an internal concept of a psychological intervention and to participate in efforts involving the acquisition of concrete resources. Mental health therapeutic assistance can be provided after people have been educated and have developed appropriate expectations of what mental health efforts can contribute to others, such as care givers and victims. By their efforts and the repertoire of behaviors displayed, mental health workers can reinforce the importance of the newly emerging mental health role in disaster assistance during the third stage.

The roles started in the temporary shelters can be used as a foundation to build a co-professional collaborative role. For example, the relationship with Red Cross team leaders, who are the same in the temporary housing and the one-stop centers as they were in the temporary shelters, may continue on a collaborative and sharing basis, but the relationship changes in strategy and responsibility. As the agencies come to know each other better, arrangements can be made and modified on how the mental health worker is to function and which mental health techniques are useful to other professionals. Improvements can be made accordingly, and changes in interactive procedures can be adopted on a trial basis. This area of collaboration is so new that few guidelines are available.

The same type of negotiations will have to be developed with the leader, generally a federal administrator, of the central FEMA office. Generally, this administrator will have had little experience in crisis counseling or dealing with mental health work focused on a certain population. It is helpful to have links with this administrator to reinforce the position that all mental health activies are a part of the federal assistance offered to a population after a disaster.

A staff intervention approach to assist the victim follows the case manager model for dealing with a stressed individual's life situation. The objective is to bring together resources that will support and assist the victim's ability to cope and find solutions to problems. Within this managing role, the mental health worker must incorporate the roles of planner, linker, and convener of resources while participating with the health and postdisaster intervention operations which, by this time, have changed location, objectives, amounts of resources available, and personnel.

State and federal resources mobilized to help reconstruct homes and neighborhoods continue to be crucial in attending to the mental health problems presented by victims. Important linkages must be established between mental health leaders and planners, managers, and members at the higher administrative levels of public and private agencies. Many problem-solving approaches depend on the amounts of concrete resources and assistance available to the victims.

Major communication problems, misrepresentations, and delays between resources offered and services delivered to homeless victims are an additional and important part of recurring grief in the postdisaster crisis. Active and systematic collaboration between all levels of official representatives and the mental health workers promotes an effective and efficient use of support systems for the victims. The continuous need for documentation and communication between different agency members reinforces the role of the mental health people as intervenors and assisting members of the overall disaster aid team. Difficulties often arise in collaboration, coordination, and interpretation of documentation language; these problems are symbolic stressors to the victims and further interfere with crisis resolution. The difficulties must be analyzed and new procedures developed to find solutions. This can be facilitated by researching issues of confidentiality and regulations mandating exchange of information. Discussions and acceptance of certain areas of collaborative exchange will help the mental health worker develop community support systems to aid victims. These exchanges are frequently limited by social and/or legal constraints that impede cooperative endeavors.

SKILLS TO PRACTICE

The necessary repertoire of mental health intervention techniques increases as different aims, objectives, and psychological levels of intervention are identified. Because the tempo of disaster service activity changes eventually, usually after several weeks, new planning can take place. Reflecting on and choosing options for action while having more time for interventions promotes the use of known therapy modalities. Changes in the physical and social environment, the emotional state of the victims, and the organization of disaster assistance agency structures from the first hours in the shelters will influence the choice of different approaches in mental health intervention. The stability of the victims' living arrangements within various housing settings continues to shift, and the pace of their requests for assistance slows down and becomes irregular. Each family appears to have different specific needs and different presenting problems. These particular fluctuating changes manifest themselves as variations of crisis phenomenology behavior. The mental health workers at this stage work with individual families, tailoring their services according to the type and amount of other assistance already given and according to the level of psychological resources available to the mental health team.

The following example highlights these issues. This case involves a family of four in which the husband contacted a crisis counselor:

> The husband was a 59-year-old unemployed auto mechanic. He lived with his 55-year-old wife and two daughters in their late teens. During the storm, their home was flooded and they were evacuated. Initially they were placed in a school designated as a disaster shelter. This was followed by a move to a motel for six weeks, after which they were able to move in with relatives until their house could be repaired.
>
> Initial contact was established with the crisis counselor by visiting the outreach office. The husband was the key member of the family who initiated

and followed through on contacts and who manifested symptoms of tension, suspiciousness, anger, and occasional loss of impulse control. The other members of the family complained of fatigue, depression, sleep problems, and trouble in daily task activities. These behavior patterns seemed to be related to their sense of frustration and impatience about the repair of their home.

While assisting the family members in checking on all their forms, the worker began to inquire about some of the experiences the family had undergone since the storm and asked questions concerning the evacuation and their living situation. As the four individuals tried to remember and relate what had happened, they became more visibly agitated and tense. The father had to leave the room for a short time to calm himself. The wife told the worker that her husband had a history of hypertension and seemed to lose control easily and react with anger, becoming immobilized by his emotional and physical state. She believed that the problems brought about by the damaged house, their evacuation, and the way they had to live were aggravating his health. He lost his "cool" when he accompanied an inspector to check the damaged house prior to beginning the work necessary to make the house safe once more.

The worker was able to assess that the husband needed crisis counseling immediately. He also offered support to the other family members but concentrated in his meetings on the issues presented by the husband. He proceeded to offer help with some of the bureaucratic steps in obtaining the right resources and also embarked on a short-term crisis resolution therapy with the father. After five weeks this involvement began to taper off as the psychological symptoms of crisis diminished. The client acknowledged feeling much better, and meetings were scheduled for once a month.

One day the client appeared at the office with a problem concerning his application for a repair loan. As technical assistance was again offered, it was evident that this event had rekindled the angry reaction of the victim. By the intensity of the emotional reaction the client was having toward the situation confronting him, the worker picked up the cues learned from the previous counseling and rapidly set up a therapeutic alliance to solve this problem. However, the therapeutic attachment sometimes conflicted with the client's need to make decisions and act independently. This need was met by offering options with specific objectives and expected outcomes within a certain time frame. This approach was seen as useful by the victim, who recovered through this process a sense of orientation and capability.

Once again, as the perceived crisis proportion of the new event abated, the worker became less active with the family. Periodic checks by the worker demonstrated that things were going fairly well, and the client was taking some initiative for keeping the family affairs in relative balance. They finally moved into their house and on the last check appeared to be back to their usual functioning.

In this last phase, with increased mobilization, the potential for educating larger numbers of volunteers and mental health professionals to continue helping emerges as a possibility. The small mental health team that generally starts in a shelter gets more members by the active involvement of other mental health professionals who become interested and offer time in the assistance operations. The possibility of practicing short-term therapy, helping couples and families, and starting group therapy becomes more feasible. At the same time, crisis intervention, counseling, and referrals to backup services within mental health clinics or hospitals continue. The skills practiced to form the linkages and collaborations with other agencies begin to recede as a primary activity. Although the need to manage resources and to collaborate with other agencies still exists, the psychodynamic characteristics of the cases that remain in the community appear to be more complex and more extensive. At this time, psychopathology symptoms will be displayed, rather than the short-term dysfunction and overwhelming "postdisaster syndrome" found during the first days.

The fact that families are relocated farther out into various distant communities, while agency members return to their own central, separate offices in different parts of a city, creates both physical and psychological distance, as well as a time barrier. Unless good linkages have been established from the beginning, this adds to the psychological and concrete problems associated with assisting victims. Busy phone lines continue to be a problem, and mental health workers find themselves not only assisting the victims in psychologically processing postdisaster symptoms, but also helping them cope with the added frustration caused by delays or mix-ups in getting concrete help.

Mental health workers must also intervene if victims continue to be unable, because of emotional problems, to communicate their recurring housing or job needs to other agencies. Bureaucratic problems of communication and decision making, problems with disaster agency workers who are often unavailable to help, or problems with misplaced or delayed authorization documents all serve to reinforce and aggravate postdisaster emotional instability and add stress, which has just begun to be resolved by the therapeutic intervention of the crisis counselor. The phenomenon of victims backing over and over again into despair, frustration, and depression, after experiencing a hopeful sense of resolution, creates a continuous area of psychological work to which the mental health workers must become sensitive. A worker must develop skills to differentiate among the phenomenological levels of naturally occurring mourning, crisis, adaptation, and reality behavior caused by impatience and frustration.

Although each stage of assistance has its difficulties, this last stage is particularly hard as victims who have been housed in temporary shelters return to their own disrupted or fragmented world and family. The victims are now faced with the uphill battle of organizing their lives, jobs, or disrupted pasts. They are trying to make these adjustments while still operating under extreme emotional tension and fatigue, and while still caught up in phases of mourning. Individuals who are unable to function at levels of accustomed behavior continue to be identified by care givers. Conversely, some persons are able to be task oriented in their daily lives. They have developed adequate coping skills and have resigned themselves to dealing with the painful experience of the disaster and the traumatic experience of many moves. However, the task of readapting is further complicated if there has been the loss of loved ones or of important personal real estate property such as shops, clinics, or offices.

Emotional reactions are presented at different levels of severity when dealing with the last phases of mourning processes and their sequels. Recognizing the appropriate phenomenology, in order to identify and ascertain the phase of mourning, and knowing how much assistance to give through an "ego-auxiliary" approach are two of the skills necessary to understand the level of resolution victims have reached at this time.

Table 2 charts the areas of concern through the phases of disaster, in constructing a plan to meet the mental health needs of disaster victims. It depicts the interphasing of key issues facing mental health workers as they try to gather professional resources, deploy them, and actively apply their skills. It points out how specific activities are phase focused within a developmental unfolding of psychological needs, rescue and relief operations, and crisis resolution with its adaptation outcome. The figure presents the beginning and end points of active assistance. It shows that all activities must be interrelated, and it sets up the proposition that a certain percentage of crisis outcomes will last a longer time than previously expected.

CONCLUSION

This handbook presents the basic and applied knowledge of the effects of a disaster on human behavior. It is an attempt by the authors to assemble, organize, and present the type of knowledge known to the field and to document fruitful intervention techniques for mental health professionals who will be called upon to assist disaster victims.

This is still a pioneering area of mental health intervention, but already it offers glimpses of how basic research in the fields of biology, brain chemistry, psychosomatic medicine, behavior models, and crisis intervention could enhance and offer future methodology in intervention.

The handbook analyzes the role of mental health workers and also identifies a series of new roles, which still need further clarification and definition. Mental health professionals will have to participate at the planning level with key government leaders in both federal and state

Table 2. Postdisaster Planning and Intervention for Mental Health Workers

	Phase I	Phase II	Phase III
Planning Operations	Activate decision to assist Enter field of action Get data on disaster assistance Develop linking procedures	Identify leadership role Develop direction and management of operations Reinforce further links with new disaster assistance groups Select and acquire physical area for mental health operations	Continue to meet systematically and participate continually with ongoing and long-term planning
Consultation and Education	Develop collaborative and participatory relations with disaster assistance groups Develop joint procedures with Red Cross staff Offer technical assistance to medical professionals Participate with the educational media through TV, newspapers, radio, and community activities	Develop and negotiate consultation relations with disaster assistance agencies Participate and collaborate with agency procedures (HUD, FEMA, etc.) Link disparate and fragmented human services	
Psychological Intervention Objectives: Process Techniques Function Roles Level of responsibility taken	Develop procedures (intake, documentation, confidentiality, referral system, closure of cases, access to documentation, storing of documentation, etc.) "Triage" First-aid assistance Counseling and support Guidance and advice	Outreach: Crisis counseling Comprehensive assistance Advocacy: Referral to clinic or hospital Short-term therapy Clarification and education Assistance to obtain resources	Close cases Monitor acceptance of referral Check closed cases that had special problems Offer linking to further services if individual wants or needs them Follow-through

agencies. They can educate and consult in the early emergency development of resources, when rapid decision making can offer the best possibility of intervention based on knowledge of group psychology and psychophysiologic reactions. This will necessitate increased knowledge in planning and needs assessment techniques. It is a new field for mental health professionals, who will collaborate with civil defense, Red Cross, emergency preparedness, and similar agencies. Other skills and approaches are also new in the area of consultation, education, and working with the public media. New use of technology in rapid communication and transportation, which is being incorporated into disaster assistance planning, will have to be incorporated into mental health intervention techniques as well.

Finally, this new methodology for psychological assistance to victims of disasters needs to be researched to evaluate the most effective and cost-efficient way of applying it. Not enough resources will be available in the immediate future to assist the large numbers of traumatized individuals suffering from the effects of both man-made and natural disasters. Thus we need to learn methods of intervention that both control and prevent devastating psychological after-effects from the loss and trauma that accidentally shatter the lives of unlucky individuals.

BIBLIOGRAPHY

Ahearn, Federico L. *Consecuencias Psico-Sociales de un Terremoto.* Managua, Nicaragua: Junta Nacional de Asistencia y Previsión, 1976.

Ahearn, Federico L., and Castellón, Rizo S. "Problemas de salud mental despues de una situación de desastre." *Boletín* 85 (1978):1-15.

Anderson, John W. "Cultural Adaptation to Threatened Disaster." *Human Organizations* 27 (1968):298-307.

Balzevic, D.; Durrigl, V.; Miletic, J.; Sartorius, N.; Stary, D.; Saric, M.; and Vidjen, R. "Psychic Reactions to a Natural Disaster." *Lijecnicki Vjesnik* 89 (1967):907-21.

Barton, Allen H. *Communities in Disaster: A Sociological Analysis of Collective Stress Situations.* New York: Doubleday, Anchor Books, 1970.

Bates, Frederick L. et al. *The Social and Psychological Consequences of a Natural Disaster.* Washington, D.C.: National Academy of Sciences-National Research Council, Publication 1081, 1963.

Bennet, Glin. "Bristol Floods 1968. Controlled Survey of Effects on Health of Local Community Disaster." *British Medical Journal* 3 (1970):454-58.

Birnbaum, Freda; Coplon, Jennifer; and Scharff, Ira. "Crisis Intervention after a Natural Disaster." *Social Casework* 54 (1973):545-51.

Block, Donald A.; Silber, Earle; and Perry, Stewart. "Some Factors in the Emotional Reaction of Children to Disaster." Bethesda, Md.: Laboratory of Child Research, National Institute of Mental Health, 1953.

Bolin, Robert. "Family Recovery from Natural Disaster." *Mass Emergencies* 1 (1976):267-77.

Bowlby, John. "Process of Mourning." *International Journal of Psycho-analysis* 42 (1961):310-20.

Burke, Edmund M. *A Participatory Approach to Urban Planning.* New York: Human Sciences Press, 1979.

Caplan, Gerald. *Support Systems in Community Mental Health.* New York: Behavioral Publications, 1974.

Church, June. "The Buffalo Creek Disaster: Extent and Range of Emotional and/or Behavioral Problems." Paper for APA Symposium on Picking up the Pieces: Disaster Intervention and Human Ecology, Montreal, Canada, 1973.

Cohen, Raquel E. "Post-Disaster Mobilization of a Crisis Intervention Team: The Managua Experience." In *Emergency and Disaster Management: A Mental Health Source Book,* edited by H. J. Parad, H.L.P. Resnick, and L. G. Parad. Bowie, Md.: Charles Press, 1976.

Crawshaw, Ralph. "Reactions to a Disaster." *Archives of General Psychiatry* 9 (1963):157-62.

Dade County Department of Civil Defense. "Hurricane David." Report. Miami, Fla., January 21, 1980.

de Ville de Goyet, C. "El Terremoto de Guatemala: Evaluación Epidemiológica de las Operaciones de Socorro." *Boletín* 81 (1976).

Dimsdale, Joel E. "The Coping Behavior of Nazi Concentration Camp Survivors." *American Journal of Psychiatry* 131 (1974): 792-97.

_____. "Emotional Causes of Sudden Death." *American Journal of Psychiatry* 134 (1977):1361-66.

"Disaster Epidemiology." Editorial in *The International Journal of Epidemiology* 4 (1975): 5-7.

Dohrenwend, Bruce S., and Dohrenwend, Barbara P. "Some Issues in Research on Stressful Life Events." *Journal of Nervous Mental Disorders* 166: (1978): 7-15.

_____. *Stressful Life Events: Their Nature and Effects.* New York: John Wiley and Sons, 1974.

Drabek, Thomas E. "Social Processes in Disaster: Family Evacuations." *Social Problems* 16 (1969): 336-49.

Drabek, Thomas E., and Boggs, Keith S. "Families in Disaster: Reactions and Relatives." *Journal of Marriage and the Family* 30 (1968):443-51.

Drabek, Thomas E., and Key, William H. "The Impact of Disaster on Primary Group Linkages." *Mass Emergencies* 1 (1976):89-105.

Drabek, Thomas E.; Key, William H.; Erickson, Patricia E.; and Crowe, Juanita L. "Longitudinal Impact of Disaster on Family Functioning." Final report to National Institute of Mental Health for grant no. R01MH15425, 1973.

Drabek, Thomas E. et al. "The Impact of Disaster on Kin Relationships." *Journal of Marriage and the Family* 37 (1975):481-94.

Drayer, Calvin. "Psychological Factors and Problems, Emergency and Long-Term." *The Annals* 309 (1957):151-59.

Drayer, Calvin; Cameron, D. C.; Woodward, W. D.; and Glass, Albert J. "Psychological First Aid in Community Disasters." Washington, D.C.: American Psychiatric Association, 1954.

Dynes, Russell R. *Organized Behavior in Disaster.* Columbus: Ohio State University, Disaster Research Center, book and monograph series no. 3, 1973.

Dynes, Russell R.; Quarantelli, Enrico L.; and Kreps, Gary A. *A Perspective on Disaster Planning.* Columbus: Ohio State University, Disaster Research Center, report series no. 11, 1972.

Erikson, Kai T. *Everything in Its Path.* New York: Simon and Schuster, 1976.

_____. "Loss of Communality at Buffalo Creek." *American Journal of Psychiatry* 133 (1976):302-4.

Erikson, Patricia; Drabek, Thomas E.; Key, William H.; and Crowe, Juanita L. "Families in Disaster." *Mass Emergencies* 1 (1976):206-13.

Executive Office of the President, Office of Emergency Preparedness. *The Federal Response to Tropical Storm Agnes,* Washington, D.C., 1973.

Farber, Irving J. "Psychological Aspects of Mass Disasters." *Journal of the National Medical Association* 59 (1967):340-45.

Fogleman, Charles, and Parenton, V. J. "Disaster and Aftermath. Selected Aspects of Individual and Group Behavior in Critical Situation." *Social Forces* 38

(1959):129-35.

Form, William H., and Nosow, Sigmund. *Community in Disaster.* New York: Harper and Bros., 1958.

Frederick, Calvin J. "Current Thinking About Crises or Psychological Intervention in United States Disasters." *Mass Emergencies* 2 (1977):43-50.

————. "Psychological First Aid: Emergency Mental Health and Disaster Assistance." *The Psychotherapy Bulletin* 10 (1977):15-20.

Fried, Marc. "Grieving for a Lost Home." In *The Urban Condition,* edited by Leonard Dahl. New York: Basic Books, 1963.

Friedsam, H. J. "Older Persons in Disasters." In *Man and Society in Disaster,* edited by G. W. Baker and D. W. Chapman. New York: Basic Books, 1962.

Fritz, Charles E. "Disaster." In *Contemporary Social Problems,* edited by R. K. Merton and R. A. Nisbet. New York: Harcourt, Brace, and World, 1966.

————. "Disasters Compared in Six American Communities." *Human Organization* 16 (1967):6-9.

Fritz, Charles E., and Marks, Eli A. "The NORC Studies of Human Behavior in Disaster." *Journal of Social Issues* 10 (1954): 26-41.

Fritz, Charles E., and Williams, Harry B. "The Human Being in Disaster." *The Annals* 309 (1957): 42-51.

Gellman, Woody, and Jackson, Barbara, *Disaster Illustrated.* New York: Harmony Books, 1976.

Glass, Albert J. "Psychological Aspects of Disaster." *Journal of the American Medical Association* 171 (1959):222.

Goldstein, Arnold. "Reactions to Disaster." *Psychiatric Communications* 3 (1960): 47-58.

Gottlieb, B. J. "The Contribution of Natural Support Systems and Primary Prevention among Four Social Subgroups of Adolescence Males." *Adolescence* 10 (1975):207-20.

Grosser, F. H.; Wechsler, H.; and Greenblatt, M., eds. *The Threat of Impending Disaster: Contributions to the Psychology of Stress.* Cambridge, Mass.: MIT Press, 1964.

Gut, Emmy. "Some Aspects of Adult Mourning." *Omega* 15 (1974):323-42.

Hall, Philip S., and Landreth, Patrick W. "Assessing Some Long-Term Consequences of a Natural Disaster." *Mass Emergencies* 1 (1975):55-61.

Hammer, Muriel. "Influences of Small Social Networks as Factors on Mental Health Admission." *Human Organization* 22 (1963):243-51.

Harshbarger, Dwight. "An Ecological Perspective on Disastrous and Facilitative Disaster Intervention Based on the Buffalo Creek Disaster." Paper presented at the National Institute of Mental Health Continuing Education Seminar on Emergency Health Services, Washington, D.C., 1973.

————. "Picking up the Pieces: Disaster Intervention and Human Ecology." *Omega* 5 (1974):55-59.

Healy, Richard J. *Emergency and Disaster Planning.* New York: John Wiley and Sons, 1969.

Hill, R. and Hansen, D. A. "Families in Disaster." In *Man and Society in Disaster,* edited by G. W. Baker and D. W. Chapman. New York: Basic Books, 1962.

Howard, Stephen J., and Godron, Norma S. *Final Progress Report: Mental Health Intervention in a Major Disaster.* Van Nuys, Calif., research grant no. MHZ1649-01, 1972.

Janis, Irving L. *Psychological Stress.* New York: John Wiley and Sons, 1958.

Janney, J. G.; Masuda, M.; and Holmes, T. H. "Impact of a Natural Catastrophe on Life Events." *Journal of Human Stress* 3 (1977):22-34.

Jerí, Raul. "Problemas de Conducta en los Desastres." *Acta Medica Peruana* 3 (1974):37-48.

Kastenbaum, Robert. "Disaster, Death, and Human Ecology." *Omega* 5 (1974): 65-72.

Kilpatrick, F. P. "Problems of Perception in Extreme Situations." *Human Organization* 16 (1957):20-22.

Kinston, Warren, and Rosser, Rachel. "Disaster: Effects on Mental and Physical State." *Journal of Psychosomatic Research* 18 (1974):437-56.

Knaus, R. L. "Crisis Intervention in a Disaster Area: The Pennsylvania Flood in Wilkes-Barre." *Journal of the American Osteopathic Association* 75 (1975): 297-301.

Kübler-Ross, Elisabeth. *On Death and Dying.* New York: Macmillan, 1970.

Lazarus, Richard S. "Psychological Stress and Coping in Adaptation and Illness." *International Journal of Psychiatry and Medicine* 5 (1974):321-33.

Leopold, R. L., and Dillon, Harold. "Psycho-Anatomy of Disaster." *American Journal of Psychiatry* 119 (1963):913-21.

Lifton, Robert J. *Death in Life: Survivors of Hiroshima.* Los Angeles: S and S Enterprises, 1967.

Lifton, Robert J., and Olson, Eric. "The Human Meaning of Total Disaster: The Buffalo Creek Experience." *Psychiatry* 39 (1976):1-18.

Lindemann, Erich. *Beyond Grief: Studies in Crisis Intervention,* edited by Elizabeth Lindemann. New York: Jason Aronson, 1979.

_____. "Symptomatology and Management of Acute Grief." *American Journal of Psychiatry* 101 (1944):141-48.

Logue, James Nicholas. "Long-Term Effects of a Major Natural Disaster. The Hurricane Agnes Flood in the Wyoming Valley of Pennsylvania, June 1972." Ph.D. dissertation, Columbia University, 1976.

McGee, Richard K. *The Role of Crisis Intervention Services in Disaster Recovery.* Gainesville: University of Florida, 1973.

McGonagle, L. C. "Psychological Aspects of Disaster." *American Journal of Public Health* 54 (1964):638-43.

Marks, Eli. S. et al. *Human Reactions in Disaster Situations.* Chicago: University of Chicago, National Opinion Research Center, 1954.

Marris, Peter. *Loss and Change.* New York: Anchor Books, 1975.

Melick, M. E. *Social Psychological and Medical Aspects of Stress-Related Illness In the Recovery Period of a Natural Disaster.* Unpublished doctoral dissertation, State University of New York at Albany, 1976.

Moore, Harry Estill. "Some Emotional Concomitants of Disaster." *Mental Hygiene* 42 (1958):45-50.

_____. "Toward a Theory of Disaster." *American Sociological Review* 21 (1956):733-37.

Moore, Harry Estill, and Friedsam, H. J. "Reported Emotional Stress Following a Disaster." *Social Forces* 38 (1959):135-39.

Morris, Jack H. "Survival Syndrome." *Wall Street Journal,* January 4, 1974, p. 1.

Mussari, A. J. *Appointment with Disaster: The Swelling of the Flood.* Wilkes-Barre, Pa.: Northeast Publishers, 1974.

Okura, K. P. "Mobilizing in Response to a Major Disaster." *Community Mental Health Journal* 11 (1975):136-44.

Parad, H. J., ed. *Crisis Intervention: Selected Readings.* New York: Family Service Association of America, 1965.

Parad, H. J.; Resnick, H.L.P.; and Parad, L. G. *Emergency and Disaster Management.* Bowie, Md.: Charles Press, 1976.

Parker, G. "Cyclone Tracy and Darwin Evacuees: On the Restoration of the Species." *British Journal of Psychiatry* 130 (1977):548-55.

Pearlin, Leonard I., and Schooler, Carmi. "The Structure of Coping." *Journal of Health and Social Behavior* 19 (1978):2-21.

Penick, Elizabeth C.; Larcen, Stephen W.; and Powell, Barbara J. *Final Report: Lt. Governor's Task Force for Mental Health Delivery Systems in Times of Disaster.* St. Louis, Mo.: St. Louis State Hospital, 1974.

Penick, Elizabeth C.; Powell, B. J.; and Sieck, W. A. "Mental Health Problems and Natural Disaster: Tornado Victims." *Journal of Community Psychology* 4 (1976):64-68.

Perrow, Charles. "A Framework for the Comparative Analysis of Organization." *American Sociological Review* 32 (1967):194-208.

Perry, Ronald W., and Lindell, M. K. "The Psychological Consequences of Natural Disaster: A Review of Research on American Communities." *Mass Emergencies* 3 (1978):105-15.

Pines, Ayala, and Maslack, Christina. "Characteristics of Staff Burnout in Mental Health Settings." *Hospital and Community Psychiatry* 29 (1978):233-37.

Popovíc, M., and Petrovíc, D. "After the Earthquake." *Lancet* 7370 (1964): 1169-71.

Poulshock, S. Walter, and Cohen, Elias S. "The Elderly in the Aftermath of a Disaster." *The Gerontologist* 15 (1975):357-61.

Quarantelli, Enrico L. "The Community General Hospital: Its Immediate Problems in Disasters." *American Behavioral Scientist* 13 (1970):380-91.

_____. "Images of Withdrawal Behavior in Disaster: Some Misconceptions." *Social Problems* 8 (1960):68-79.

Quarantelli, Enrico L., and Dynes, Russell, R. *Images of Disaster Behavior: Myths and Consequences.* Columbus: Ohio State University, Disaster Research Center, preliminary paper no. 5, 1972.

_____. *Operational Problems of Organizations in Disasters.* Emergency Operations Symposium. Santa Monica, Calif.: System Development Corporation, 1967.

_____. "Organizational and Group Behavior in Disasters." *American Behavioral Scientist* 13 (1970):325-46.

_____. "Response to Social Crisis and Disaster." *Annual Review of Sociology* 3 (1977):23-49.

_____. "When Disaster Strikes (It isn't much like what you've heard about)." *Psychology Today* 5 (1972):66-70.

Rangell, L. "Discussion of the Buffalo Creek Disaster: The Course of Psychic Trauma." *American Journal of Psychiatry* 133 (1976):313-16.

Rochlin, Gregory. *Griefs and Discontents: The Faces of Change.* Boston: Little,

Brown and Co., 1965.

Schulberg, Herbert C. "Disaster, Crisis Theory and Intervention Strategies." *Omega* 5 (1974):77-87.

Selye, Hans. "General Physiology and Pathology of Stress." In *Fifth Annual Report on Stress 1955-56,* edited by Hans Selye and G. Heuser. New York: MD Publishers, 1956.

_____. *The Stress of Life.* McGraw-Hill, 1956.

Shneidman, Edwin. "Deathwork and Stages of Aging." In *Death: Current Perspectives,* edited by Edwin Shneidman. Palo Alto, Calif.: Mayfield, 1976.

Snyder, Solomon H., M.D. "The Opiate Receptor and Morphine-Like Peptides in the Brain." *American Journal of Psychiatry* 135 (1978):645-52.

Speck, R. V., and Rueveni, U. "Network Therapy: A Developing Concept." *Family Process* 8 (1969):182-91.

Sterling, Joyce; Drabek, Thomas; and Key, William. "The Long-Term Effects of Disaster on the Health Self-Perceptions of Victims." Paper read at meetings of American Sociological Association, Chicago, Ill., 1977.

Stern, G. M. "Disaster at Buffalo Creek: From Chaos to Responsibility." *American Journal of Psychiatry* 133 (1976):300-301.

Taylor, James B.; Lucker, Louis A.; and Key, William. *Tornado: A Community Response to Disaster.* Seattle: University of Washington Press, 1970.

Taylor, Verta A. "Good News About Disaster." *Psychology Today* 11 (1977): 93-94, 124-26.

Taylor, Verta A. et al. *Delivery of Mental Health Services in Disasters: The Xenia Tornado and Some Implications.* Columbus: Ohio State University, Disaster Research Center, book and monograph series no. 11, 1976.

Tierney, Kathleen J., and Baisden, Barbara. *Crisis Intervention Programs for Disaster Victims: A Source Book and Manual for Smaller Communities.* U.S. Department of Health, Education, and Welfare publication no. (ADM) 79-675, 1979.

Titchener, James L., and Kapp, Frederic T. "Family and Character Change at Buffalo Creek." *American Journal of Psychiatry* 133 (1976):295-99.

Tolsdorf, Christopher C. "Social Networks, Support, and Coping." *Family Process* 15 (1976):407-17.

Tuckman, Alan J. "Disaster and Mental Health Intervention." *Community Mental Health Journal* 9 (1973):151-57.

Tyhurst, J. S. "Individual Reactions to Community Disaster: The Natural History of Psychiatric Phenomena." *American Journal of Psychiatry* 107 (1951):23-27.

_____. "Psychological and Social Aspects of Civilian Disaster." *Canadian Medical Association Journal* 76 (1957a):385-93.

Wallace, Anthony F. C. "Mazeway Disintegration." *Human Organization* 16 (1957):23-27.

_____. "Tornado in Worcester: An Explanatory Study of Individual and Community Behavior in an Extreme Situation." Washington, D.C.: Committee on Disaster Studies, study no. 3. National Academy of Science, National Research Council publication no. 392, 1956.

Wenger, Dennis E.; Dykes, James D.; Sphak, Thomas B.; and Neff, Joan L. "It's a Matter of Myths: An Empirical Examination of Individual Insight into Disaster Responses." *Mass Emergencies* 1 (1975):33-46.

White, Robert W. "Strategies of Adaptation: An Attempt at Systematic Description." *Coping and Adaptation,* edited by George V. Coehlo; David A. Hamburg; and John E. Adams. New York: Basic Books, 1974.

Williams, Harry B., and Fritz, Charles. "The Human Being in Disaster: A Research Perspective." *The Annals* 309 (1957):42-51.

Wilson, Robert N. "Disaster and Mental Health," In *Man and Society in Disaster,* edited by G. W. Baker and D. S. Chapman. New York: Basic Books, 1962.

Wolff, Harold G., M.D. *Stress and Disease.* Springfield, Ill.: Charles C. Thomas, 1953.

Wolfstein, M. *Disaster: A Psychological Essay.* Glencoe, Ill.: The Free Press, 1957.

Yandon, B., and Chetkow, B. H. "Short-Term Intervention: A Model of Emergency Services for Times of Crisis." *Mental Health Sociology* 3 (1976):33-52.

Zarle, Thomas H.; Hartsough, Don M.; and Ottinger, Donald R. "Tornado Recovery: The Development of a Professional-Paraprofessional Response to a Disaster." *Journal of Community Psychology* 2 (1974):311-20.

INDEX

Lightning Source UK Ltd.
Milton Keynes UK
UKOW02f1115230616

276909UK00001B/290/P